Leigh,

Be joyful always
pray continually
give thanks in
all circumstances
for this is God's will
for you in Christ Jesus

1 Thessalonians
5:16-18

your Sister
in
Christ
Cindy

HAVING *Joy* IN THE MIDST OF THE STORM

Through The Storm He Is Lord, Lord Of All

CINDY ORIOL

WESTBOW
PRESS®
A DIVISION OF THOMAS NELSON
& ZONDERVAN

Scriptures taken from the Holy Bible, New International Version®, NIV®.
Copyright © 1973, 1978, 1984, 2011 by Biblica, Inc.™ Used by permission
of Zondervan. All rights reserved worldwide. www.zondervan.com The
"NIV" and "New International Version" are trademarks registered in
the United States Patent and Trademark Office by Biblica, Inc.™

WestBow Press books may be ordered through booksellers or by contacting:

WestBow Press
A Division of Thomas Nelson & Zondervan
1663 Liberty Drive
Bloomington, IN 47403
www.westbowpress.com
1 (866) 928-1240

ISBN: 978-1-9736-5792-7 (sc)
ISBN: 978-1-9736-5791-0 (e)

Print information available on the last page.

WestBow Press rev. date: 04/01/2019

CONTENTS

Preface xiii

Author Notes xvii

Prologue.. xix

1 Jesus Takes Away Our Fears 1

2 Jesus Performs Miracles 24

3 Jesus Is Our Hope.................................. 38

4 Jesus Is The Prince Of Peace 51

5 Jesus Is Love 68

6 Jesus Is The Light 92

7 Jesus Is Our Strength...........................107

8 Jesus Is The Way, The Truth And The
   Life..126

9 Jesus Is Forever 146

Endorsements

Don Waddell & Larry Garwood & Judy Gerdis

I served in the military for 28 years and flew combat in Vietnam. That said, I have known few individuals with the courage and commitment of Cindy Oriol. She has courageously battled a half dozen diseases any one of which would defeat most people. Yet her faith and commitment to her Lord has remained strong and served as an inspiration to me and others who know her. I'm sure her book will inspire you as well.

- Don Waddell USAF Retired

To the Reader of HAVING JOY IN THE MIDST OF THE STORM:

Many years ago, when I was a budding adolescent, a very wise English Literature teacher provided some excellent advice – when our class seemed to be at a loss for subjects upon which to base our assignment to write a short story.

She admonished that writing is always done best when the author writes about a subject that they actually know something about and perhaps have even experienced first-hand.

Since Cindy Oriol is significantly younger than I, it stands to reason that she was not in that class. Nevertheless, this is exactly what she has done in this book which can and will provide a rich source of strength, stamina, courage and thus encouragement to those who are hurting and feeling discourage – for any reason – in their life journey.

Although many of her own person life experiences might be categorized as devastating by the outsider looking at her life, Cindy has always seen her many struggles as a means of drawing closer to the Lord that she so desperately loves and believes in. Her steadfast trust in Him and love for Him and other of this human race will jump off the pages and perhaps provide you with a greater means of improving those facets of your own life – by learning to utilize and cultivate these and other very positive character traits which are found in the words of this book.

Knowing Cindy as I do, this would certainly be her desire for you.

-Larry A. Garwood
Lay Pastor for the Classic Worship Family at Southeast Christian Church and Management Consultant Specializing in Risk and Crisis Management

I've known Cindy for a short time but she has an amazing story. And, like she would say, God's not finished with her yet! There are some people who seem to float through life with little problems. I'm sure Cindy would have pity on them because it is in the valley that you smell the sweet fragrance of the Holy Spirit and his comforting arms. Having more sick days than well in the last six years, makes her an expert in trusting God. Even at her lowest Cindy has learned to praise and give thanks in all things. Her book will give you a blueprint to follow "when" your day comes to hold on tight and live victoriously.

Judy Gerdis
Author of GET IN THE BOAT!
Facilitator of Cancer Care – Southeast Christian Warrior

Dedications

First and foremost I want to thank you, my Lord and Savior, for without you I am nothing. I want to thank you, Holy Spirit, for always guiding me in the right direction. You have taught me through my chronic pain, cancer, etc, that I can still put a smile on my face and find joy in the midst of the storm.

To my loving husband John, my best friend. You have been my strength while keeping me strong in my faith. There were times when I felt like throwing in the towel, but you encouraged me to keep going. You, my love, have stood by me when I was so sick that I could barely get out of bed. You are a prime example of how a Christian husband should be towards his wife. I love you, babe.

I want to thank my Cissy (Marla) for all your continued love and support. Even when I did not feel like going anywhere, you came and took me places and allowed me to cry on your shoulders. You are more than my sister in Christ, you are my "sister". You, Cissy, are the friend I prayed for when I was moving to Kentucky and I did not *know a single person. Thank you for supporting me in my writing and everything I do, I love you.*

I want to thank you, my prayer warriors, for all your love, support, and prayers. Because of the beautiful cards and your kind words, you have kept me strong and my faith increases each day. John and I would like to thank those of you who helped with transportation to my chemo treatments when John had other appointments to attend to. Thank you, Pat & Carol, for sitting with me during my chemo.

Most of all, I want to thank God the Father for loving us all so much that He sent His Son to die on the cross & raised Him up so that we would have eternal life with Him. HALLELUJAH!!!

PREFACE

I BELIEVE!

Through the many storms in my life, for which I am grateful, they have brought me closer to you, my Savior. You have shown me time after time how much you love me. I BELIEVE!

Even though I can't physically touch you, I can feel your loving arms cradling me in my weakest moments. I trust that You are there. I BELIEVE!

Even though I can not hear you, I hear the groans of your Spirit talking to me. I trust that You are there. I BELIEVE!

Even when I was wheelchair bound for nearly a year due to a life-changing injury, I trusted that You were there. I BELIEVE!

Even before You healed me from pancreatic and breast cancers, I knew You were there. I BELIEVE!

Even before You cured me from my stroke, I trusted that You were there. I BELIEVE!

Even before You protected me from getting hurt from my non-epileptic seizures and many falls, I trusted that You were there. I BELIEVE!

Even though our finances were dipping low, I trusted that You were there. I BELIEVE!

EVEN

If You did not get me out of the wheelchair and allow me to walk again with a walker or cane;

If You did not heal me from the pancreatic and breast cancer;

If You did not heal me from my stroke;

If You did not protect me from the many falls due to the seizures;

If You did not make our finances better, Lord, I do not need to see, touch, or hear You in order to believe. I have felt you pick me up and sheltered me during the storms. I have watched you perform so many miracles in my life and the life of other's. I believe in you by faith not by sight.

Lord I can not wait for your coming, when

You take me home with You for eternity. Then I will be able to see, touch, and hear You, but until then,

I BELIEVE!

AUTHOR NOTES

As I look throughout my life I can see in my darkest days – YOU WERE THERE!

When you took my daddy home with you, though I had begged you not to – YOU WERE THERE!

When I felt as if my whole world was falling apart – YOU WERE THERE!

When I couldn't hear the groaning of your Spirits voice, I knew YOU WERE THERE!

When I begged you to heal my mom from esophageal cancer, You said," No, my child, I am taking her home with me." YOU WERE THERE!

You have always been there and I could feel your loving arms cradling me as I cried out to You. You listened- YOU WERE THERE!

Lord, I am sorry for the times that I did not feel your presence or hear your voice because I thought You were not listening, when it was really me who was not listening. But, YOU WERE THERE!

PROLOGUE

My prayer for you, my readers, is that as you read my book you will see and remember those moments when Jesus comforted you during your storms as He has done in mine. These lessons have taught me to trust Him completely.

In today's crazy, mixed up world with everything bad happening all around us, we need to put our trust in Him. He is our Hope for the future, our enduring Peace, and our Strength for today.

You know if we lived in a perfect world without any trials we would not need Him. We would miss out on so many blessings like having a personal relationship with Him, the way He comforts us and showers us with love and peace, His beautiful peace. Writing "Having Joy In The Midst Of The Storm" came to me in one of the hardest trials of my life.

Please do not ever feel as if there is no hope to get us through the storms we will encounter. Jesus Christ is the hope that we need to cling to when we feel the weight of our trials pulling us beneath the sinking sand.

Romans 12:12

12 Be joyful in hope, patient in affliction, faithful in prayer.

Ephesians 3:16

16 I pray that out of his glorious riches he may strengthen you with power through his Spirit in your inner being.

He makes a way for our burdens to be lighter. When our trials are the darkest – Jesus Is The Light!

1

Jesus Takes Away Our Fears

Our Lord has performed so many miracles for my family and I. One that particularly touches my heart is the day our beautiful granddaughter Zoey was born, February 22, 2014.

Our daughter Michelle had just called us to say that her amniotic fluid was completely gone and that we needed to get to the hospital. She said that her doctor was going to induce labor. We started our two hour journey to Madison, Indiana. I was praying all the way that we would not miss Zoey's birth and that Michelle and the baby were safe. From living in Madison years ago, I knew the area pretty well, or so I thought. When we arrived there and looked around, I noticed that there were only a few cars in the parking lot and a couple of work trucks.

I jokingly said to John, "Honey, you can park anywhere that you like." As I continued to glance around the area I knew that something did not look right, so John and I walked up to the front door and read a sign. It said, "Construction work going on here." I went around to the side of the building, saw a construction worker and asked him, "What was going on here, where is the hospital? Where are all the cars?" He laughed and said," Ma'am, you are at the old hospital. They built a new one a few years ago, located up on the hill." So John and I got back into the car to search for a hospital on a hill.

We finally arrived, and after saying hello to everyone, I told them about what had just happened and we all laughed. After the laughter calmed down, we got our composure back and sat down in the waiting room anticipating the birth of our Zoey. There were so many of us that we had to take turns going in and out of Michelle's room. I was in there with her for quite sometime, I did not want to leave my baby.

Back when Michelle found out that she was going to have another baby, we all prayed to the Lord that He would bless us with a beautiful baby girl. So when she had her ultrasound to check on how well Zoey was growing she also wanted to know the sex of the baby. Our prayers were answered when we found out that the baby was a girl, we were all so ecstatic. When Zoey came out she looked just like her ultrasound picture.

We were all together in her room with our grandson Hunter, who is grandma's favorite ten year old boy in the whole world along with our son-in-law Nick. I just love to hear him call me mom because I have always wanted a son, and now I have one. When we saw how tired they were getting, we decided to give them a break so they could rest before the big event began.

We had been there for several hours when Nick came out to tell us that Michelle was going to need an emergency C- section as it was too dangerous for her to push. We found out later that Zoey's umbilical cord had completely wrapped around her neck, which made her heart rate drop very low. Because of this reason she could not descend into the birth canal.

I gathered all of us together and we immediately started praying for the both of them. I started thanking my Lord and Savior that many years ago He had blessed me with my baby girl. I came very close to losing her. I suffered a miscarriage *while carrying her two siblings. Now she was having a baby girl. I knew that both of them were in Jesus hands and that is where I left them in His loving care.*

While we were waiting, I wanted to keep our grandson Hunter occupied so he would not be worried about his mom and sister so he and I played games on the computer. I think it was called zombies. I was not sure of how to play this game but at least I kept him busy. He was so excited for his baby sister to be born and that he would finally be able to take her home.

As they were wheeling Michelle to the operating room I bent down to kiss her, told her that I loved her and that she & Zoey were in our Lord's hands. To see my baby trying to save her baby just as I did when she was born, was really rough.

Zoey arrived early in the morning weighing 6 ½ pounds. She was so alert that every time her daddy talked to her she would turn her head towards him. She also grabbed his finger whenever he put it close to her. It was such a beautiful sight to see Nick bonding with his precious baby girl. Hunter kept tapping on the window to get her attention she would look his way and he said," Look grandma, she is looking at me." This made him very happy now that he had a baby sister.

After being there for twenty hours, we were finally able to go back to Michelle's room to see her and our beautiful granddaughter. As we opened the door we witnessed such a lovely sight, Michelle holding her beautiful child sent from God. We each took a turn holding her and getting our picture taken with our adorable baby girl. Then it was time to return home as we knew the family needed rest, so reluctantly, we said our congratulations and goodbyes.

After seeing our daughter and granddaughter in such a dangerous situation, Jesus took away any fears that Satan was casting our way. Michelle told us all later that she watched the doctor remove the cord from Zoey's neck. I know that we are all miracles from God, but I believe that Zoey's birth was really special because we almost lost her due to having the umbilical cord around her little neck. but the Lord protected her and our daughter. This little girl is a bundle of happiness to us all. She has just turned four years old, with dimples and blonde hair (like mine), with a really cute voice. I want Michelle to put it in a bottle so we can hear it forever. She is always happy to see her Grandma. Children grow up so fast, we as parents and grandparents miss their cute little ways of doing things, along with other memories we hold close to our heart.

Another miracle was the day that our beautiful granddaughter, Remiah entered this world and into all of our lives. During her pregnancy, our daughter Lisa came to visit John and I several times. We made so many beautiful memories as I tried to prepare her for motherhood. Once I even gave her a pedicure, we laughed so hard I thought she was going to fall off the couch.

On October 16, 2014 Lisa called to tell us she was bleeding, she still had two more weeks till she would deliver, and was really afraid. On the drive to the hospital her dad ran every stop sign and every red light to get her there in time. We all laugh about it now, but at the time it was pretty scary. Lisa was not married at the time so Michelle and I were her coaches during her delivery. We stayed with her the whole time. We really bonded that night as mother and daughters.

Since John and I had rushed to the hospital, we hadn't eaten anything for supper yet, but I had taken two meds which resulted in a queasy feeling. I had to take my medicine that is prescribed for my chronic pain and my fibromyalgia, and taking it on an empty stomach resulted in an upset stomach.

Every time we helped Lisa to push, I would have to sit down on a wooden chair next to the bed. I kept praying to the Lord to please help me feel better. I said, "My daughter needs me," as I felt I might pass out. Eventually I started to feel better, thank you Lord!

Each time the doctor would check Lisa for dilation she would tell her to push really hard. She could feel that Remiah's head could not pass through the pelvic bone. It was stuck and was causing Lisa so much pain. What is a mother to do when she sees her child in that kind of pain. I knew that prayer was the answer, so that is what I did. I started praying Lisa's pain would stop and that Remiah would be able to descend into the birth canal.

All of a sudden Lisa was having a hard time catching her breath, not because of her contractions but because of her chest feeling heavy. She was having a panic attack and had been administered too much epidural. So they hooked her up to oxygen, which eventually calmed her breathing.

She was sweating profusely, so Michelle got a cold damp cloth and put it on her forehead. It was such a beautiful site seeing one sister taking care of the other. We were praying that Remiah would make an appearance soon.

After a little while, the doctor came in to see how many centimeters Lisa had dilated. Finally she was ten centimeters and could begin pushing again. Remiah's head still had not passed through her pelvic bone, so her doctor had to reach up inside to get her head loose. Once she had done that Lisa felt the urge to push. Her contractions were coming hard and fast.

Michelle and I both grabbed her legs to help her push the baby out. The doctor said," I can see her head, she has dark hair." Lisa pushed with everything she had and our beautiful Remiah entered this world. She had black hair and her skin looked as if she was already tanned. When the doctor put her in her mommy's arms Lisa cried buckets of tears, but happy ones, and then we all began to cry.

I had already decided that I would be staying the duration of her hospital stay. I did not want them to be alone, plus I just wanted to share this special time in Lisa and the baby's life. Of course, we did not get much sleep. Who can sleep in the hospital since every time we would start to drift off one of the lab technicians would come in to draw her labs, and the nursing assistant came in twice to take her vitals. The nursery asked us if we wanted to keep the baby in our room for the rest of the night. Lisa replied, "Yes, definitely."

She had wanted a baby for a very long time and now our Lord blessed her with her precious baby doll. We stayed for two days, and then my friend came to get us and take us back to John and I's home. During their stay Lisa regained her strength and I had some very special bonding time with Remi.

Today she is four ears old and looks just like her mommy, with her long brown hair and her beautiful smile. She can be a little shy at first, but when she gets to know you better she is very friendly. While I was taking my chemo I talked to her daily. She would say, 'Hi grandma, I love you. Are you feeling better?" We both laugh at how silly each of us looks when we face time together. Zoey and her are about the same age. They have so much fun playing with each other along with Zoey's big brother Hunter.

I am so very happy that our Lord blessed me

with these two precious bundles of joy during this time of my life. They both give me so much joy. I did not know that in a couple of months after they were born that I would need to find joy in the Lord. I was about to embark on a new journey in my life, one where I would really need a deeper relationship with the Lord. Having to learn to trust Him completely and find the strength I would need in the months and years ahead.

And So My Journey Begins

In the month of December 2014, I woke up one morning doubled over from so much pain in my abdomen. It felt as if my appendix or ovaries were going to burst, but that could not be possible since at the age of thirty three I had a total hysterectomy, and my appendix and my ovaries were also removed. What could make a person have so much pain in their organs that were no longer there. Well, you are about to find out. My meals became Jasmine rice and crackers, and I could only drink ginger-ale because everything else made my pain increase.

So, I made an appointment with my gastroenterologist. After he examined me, he said he was ordering a cat-scan on my chest, abdomen and pelvic. My test results showed two cysts on the tail of my pancreas. He decided to wait six months to see if the cysts would grow. After living with the pain for six months, he sent me for another cat-scan and it revealed that indeed, they had grown bigger.

He decided to send me to another gastroenterologist who was more advanced in this specialty field. After talking among themselves they both agreed on the next procedure of what needed to take place. The decision was that I would be going in the hospital and be put to sleep for a special procedure.

The doctor ran a scope down my esophagus, which was attached to a camera plus ultrasonic waves. He drained the fluid from the cysts to test it later. The end results were that my pancreas looked great except for the cysts. My doctors weren't that concerned, still thinking that this was normal. They had seen this happen before and usually the cysts were benign. But, because it was the pancreas, they decided to run a blood test to check my carcinoembryonic antigen. This is a test that measures the amount of protein that may appear in the areas (such as the pancreas) of some people with certain kinds of cancer. The test results showed that my numbers were very high and that I would need to see an oncologist. There was a good chance that I might have cancer.

They sent me to an oncologist that I really liked. He was a very caring doctor, one that would really take the time to address your concerns. After going over my test results, he determined that it was at least pre-cancer. He told me that my cysts were located on the tail of my pancreas, but were also lying on my spleen which would need to be removed. He also saw two small cysts on my liver and one on my kidney. He told me that they were probably benign and they were nothing to worry about.

Years ago before my relationship with Jesus, I would have been so afraid when I heard the word "Cancer" but I was not afraid now, I did not even cry. Jesus had taken away my fears. I was ready to get this surgery out of the way. I did not need to be sick, I still had too many things to do for the Lord. But, before the procedure was to take place there was an important trip to make.

In May of 2015, John and I decided to renew our wedding vows for our tenth wedding anniversary on a Florida beach, with the sun setting behind us. Our actual date is February 12, and we had originally planned to have our ceremony on February 21, (my daddy's birthday, oh, I miss him so much). But mother nature did not cooperate. We had one of the worst ice storms that Louisville, Kentucky has ever had. Snow mixed with hail and sleet. No one could go out or come down, it was too dangerous to travel.

Earlier that year, John came to tell me that because we had so many doctor bills that we wouldn't be able to have our ceremony, I cried a lot that day and a few days beyond that. So when the actual day came with the horrible storm I felt at ease because our Lord saved both John and I a lot of money from not having to buy decorations, a cake, and pay for the dance hall. We were also planning to go to Zoey's one year old birthday party. Missing her birthday celebration brought forth buckets of tears. I cried so much over missing our beautiful granddaughter's birthday.

Since John and I have relatives that reside in Florida, we thought it would be fun to ask them to celebrate with us by being a part of our ceremony. A beautiful rented condo awaited us across the road from the beach. We arrived on Friday and met up with cousin Pam and

John, her husband. I had been hoping on the way down to find a restaurant that served delicious, fresh fish, where pelicans would land on the piers where the yachts were anchored. We found a place that was perfect.

After we had finished eating our delicious meal, we decided to check into our condo. Almost immediately we all felt at home. It was so beautiful with beachy surroundings. Hanging on the walls were big, bold and colorful murals of the beach. It looked as if we were already at the ocean. Both couples had their own private bedroom. Our bed looked so comfy cozy that I wanted to jump right in and pull the covers over me. When we opened the blinds, we could see the seagulls flying all around. The mist from the ocean breeze was beckoning us to come and jump in the waves.

Before our trip, a friend of mine called and asked me if she could purchase an elegant dress for me to wear at the ceremony. I told her," Thank you that would be lovely, and I really appreciate it." It was a very thoughtful gift that she wanted to buy for me.

I tried on several dresses before coming to the perfect one. When I showed her how it looked, we both said, "Yes to the dress." It was layered with ivory lace, with rouching in the front of it that made it look very flattering with the curves of my body. It was covered with beads that shimmered with such brilliant light.

John had surprised me with a gorgeous strand of pearls that cascaded across the neck and down the back of my dress, along with long beautiful, pearl earrings to match. They were so shiny and delicate, which made my dress look more elegant. I felt so beautiful in my dress, I felt like a bride going to meet her groom with such anticipation, excitement and joy in her heart.

Ten years ago when John and I first pledged our love for each other in front of the Lord, our family, and friends we could feel His presence all around us. He is the cement that holds our marriage together. We have made Him first above everything. He took two lonely people full of the love of Him and molded them into one.

Genesis 2:23 -24

23 The man said, "This is now bone of my bones and flesh of my flesh; she shall be called 'woman,' for she was taken out of man." 24 That is why a man leaves his father and mother

and is united to his wife, and they become one flesh.

★★★★

He blessed us both when He put us together. Having Him first in every aspect of our marriage has kept us strong and faithful to each other. We keep our eyes focused on Him. He took away our fears of ever being hurt again.

I know that no one has a perfect marriage but John and I have a blessed life together. As you will read further on in this book, our love for each other and our love for our Lord continues to grow deeper each day. The days of hurting, as we were hurt in the past, are gone forever. When we have a disagreement with each other which we very seldom do, either one of us will say that we are sorry and tell the other one that we love them. Then we kiss and make up. Making up is so much fun (woo hoo!). I can honestly say that we are each other's soulmates. I do not know what I would have done without him especially during these trying times.

Our special day had finally arrived. It is funny that all the time I was getting ready I was shaking really bad, not of being fearful but just knowing that once again I was going to marry my soulmate that the Lord had given me ten years ago. I was excited, anxious and on cloud nine.

Earlier that day before the ceremony, Pam took me to shop for a wedding gift for my beloved John. I did not have much money in my wallet but I knew if the Lord wanted me to find something He would supply all my needs. As I walked down each aisle to see if I could see anything special, I said a prayer asking the Lord to bring something to my eyes and suddenly, I found myself in the house decor dept., glancing down at the pictures and frames. I felt deep in my heart that these things were not meant for me to buy, that there was something more special that I needed to find. I almost missed it, but suddenly my eyes were drawn to what the Lord wanted me to find. It was a ceramic cross that could either be hung on the wall or you could use the stand it came with. This cross was absolutely perfect. It had a tan back ground with beautiful fall flowers painted all around the cross. It was exquisite. This was definitely what the Lord wanted me to find, a cross that had the wedding vows on it. It reads like this:

> *I promise to be true to you in*
> *Good times and in bad times,*
> *In sickness and in health.*
> *I will love you*
> *And honor you*
> *All the days*
> *Of my life!*

My Lord had led me straight to the perfect gift and guess what, my readers, I had just enough money, right down to the very penny. "Praise the Lord!" He supplies all our needs.

It was now getting closer to the time when the sun would begin to set. John timed everything perfectly, we had such a fun time with a few minor mishaps. Pam's John and my John walked into each other's spots of where they were supposed to stand for the ceremony. It looked as if I was remarrying her John. Almost immediately they realized what they had done and switched back to their rightful spots. When it was the time to renew our vows John realized that he had brought the wrong card, the one he had written his vows to me was still sitting on the dining room table where he had left it. So he just told me how special I was to him and that he loved me more each day.

I do not have the words to tell you just how beautiful the beach was that night, with it's calming waves swishing up to the shore, then it would disappear slowly back into the ocean. The sand was alive with crystals of glitter. As we walked across the beach, I could feel the sand between my toes, it felt so warm and toasty. There were a few people still enjoying themselves. Some were playing Frisbee with their children, while others' were tossing the beach ball to and fro to each other. We received some lovely compliments as we walked by to get to our destination. One couple asked me what was going on, so I explained what we were about to do. They were as excited as we were, well probably not quite as excited.

All eyes were gazed upon us as we renewed our love for each other. John was trying to take some timed photos so that the camera would capture us all. Unfortunately, they did not turn out as good as we had hoped. But after the ceremony was finished, John was able to take some beautiful pictures as the sun was setting over the Gulf of

Mexico. The colors of the sky from the sinking sun, along with the reflections in the water, while some children were still playing nearby, gave us a special memory of our day.

Several people came up to greet us and wished us happiness. Some even took pictures of us on their own camera. One family took down our address so that they could mail us the photos (and they did), it was so special.

The daily weather forecast called for heavy rain that night. I knew there was no fear of our celebration being rained on because Jesus was there. We had just crossed the road and were going up the stairs to our condo when the gusty winds began to blow extremely hard. The trees were swaying back and forth so much that if a branch would have snapped off of a tree it would have hit our condo. The rain came down in huge amounts and together with the wind they acted as if they would form a tornado.

The following day as we were preparing to have some fun in the sun, John was looking around our condo and he came upon a closet full of lawn chairs, umbrellas and a selection of beach toys for children. The staff from the condo took great care of their clients and we really appreciated them.

As I was sitting on the beach writing in my journal, I heard the Spirit of the Lord speak to me. He wanted me to explain what being on the beach meant to me and how I could describe it to Him. I started journaling the magnificent surroundings. I heard the gentle peace of the waves swishing back and forth. They really touched my heart and I felt peace just like I do when I am going through a storm and Jesus is comforting me. Just like the famous picture and it's words, I saw one set of footprints in the sand because He was carrying me through the storms and trials that I have gone through and still are. Just knowing that we have a loving Savior that loves us so much that we are never alone.

As I looked down at the sand covering my feet and the water gently rushing over them, it reminded me of Jesus cleansing us of our sins when He took them to the cross with Him and because of this we are washed by the blood of the lamb, and are purified by Him. As I glanced around the sand I saw many sea shells that were broken piece by piece, just as we are, but He puts us back together and makes us whole again.

The fish are part of His creation, full of different colors and sizes just like us. He calls for all of us to be "Fishers of Men", which takes faith and determination. The sun surrounds me as it lights up the sky and warms our bodies, just as Jesus the Son covers us with warmth as we lie in His loving arms. He gives us that deep sensation of His love that only He can give.

As the sights of my vision slowly disappeared, I felt such a peace in my soul. He told me that this journal that I was writing in was going to be the beginning of our second book, and through out the pages I would give Him all the glory, honor and praise. Wow, He and I were writing another book together, I was ecstatic. We need to believe in Him by faith not by sight. I could not see Him but I knew he was there.

Tomorrow morning we would be leaving the peace and tranquility of the beach, but isn't it great to know that as long as we have Jesus the peace and tranquility will follow us everywhere. We will leave behind the seagulls hovering around and swooping down to catch a fish or two for their meal. I will miss the beautiful sounds of the waves. We were truly blessed to have this vacation.

He knew that I really needed to relax and spend some quality time with Him and John, because in two weeks after our beautiful get away, I would be having surgery on my pancreas and spleen. I believe He was making me stronger as He had already told me that it was cancer. John and I honestly never felt any fear.

"Blessed Assurance Jesus Is Mine"
We Do Believe That Jesus
Takes Away Our Fears

Genesis 26:24
26 I am the God of your father Abraham. Do not be afraid, for I am with you

Hebrews 13:6
6 So we say with confidence, The Lord is my helper; I will not be afraid. What can man do to me?

2

Jesus Performs Miracles

I had my surgery on June 8, 2015. As they wheeled me into the operating room I met a group of nurses, an anesthesiologist, and my doctor, they were all so very kind to me. However, I was freezing in there so they gave me a warm blanket. As they pulled that heated blanket over my cold body I felt the warmth right away. I told them that I had covered them with prayers for this morning, that our Lord was present and He would be helping them to do their job. They all smiled and told me," Thank you".

They put the mask over my face and told me to start counting backwards from one hundred. I think I got to 97, but before I was completely out I saw the image of Jesus in His long, white robe *with outstretched hands beckoning me to come into His loving arms, where I always felt safe.*

I was not afraid because I had been a witness to His healing powers in my life. He will perform miracles in your life too, if only you reach out to Him and tell Him what you need, but you really must believe and have faith. Our needs are not the same as His needs for us. We might pray for someone or something but when we get the results they might be totally different than what we wanted to hear, only He knows what is best for us. At other times He will give us just what we have prayed for.

I woke up in the recovery room two hours later. The first face I saw was my beloved John. He looked so handsome as he was trying to wake me up. We were so happy to see each other, he loves me just as much as I love him. He was grinning from ear to ear, and told me that he was so glad that I had made it through the surgery without any complications, then he told me that he loved me. I was ready to go home with him, but I had to remain there for four days. I was going to need healing and learn exercises to get my strength back since I was so weak from the surgery and my other health issues.

My doctor told both John and I that we should be getting the results of the biopsy back within three days. Actually they came back in two. My doctor came into the room as I was sitting on the side of the bed. I had just finished eating my breakfast, a clear-liquid diet, that consisted of ginger-ale, beef or chicken broth. I chose chicken and to top it off I had Jello(wow). I was on that diet for two days, I could not wait to have some real food. He sat down next to me and grabbed both of my hands and told me that the biopsy came back and it was cancer. This was the cancer that my Lord had already told me that I had, but that everything was going to be fine. The doctor told me that he had gotten all of the cancer, and I said," Praise the Lord."

I am truly blessed that we caught it in time and that Jesus had warned me. John and I know at least five good friends that have died from pancreatic cancer, so I asked him,"Did you see the other two cysts on my liver and the one on my kidney?" He told me that they were nowhere to be found. "Praise the Lord" for He had performed another miracle.

While he was still holding my hands he told me that "this could have only happened this way for you, Cindy, because of your faith being so strong." I thanked him, but before he left the room he reiterated once again that he had gotten all of the cancer and that I would not need any chemo or radiation, Hallelujah!

After he left, I started praising my Lord and Savior Jesus Christ. Some people might think that once the doctor left that I was alone in my room but I was not. My Jesus, my Rock, my Healer and Redeemer gave me so much comfort and reassured me that He was there with me at all times. He gave me so much strength that day and the days to follow.

I called John to tell him the news, even though he had already been planning to spend the day with me. I know I could've waited until he got there to give him the news, but I really just needed to hear his voice, I knew it would bring me comfort. He told me that he loved me and that we would get through this together because Jesus is our strength.

During my stay in the hospital several wonderful things happened, our Lord was being shown everywhere. One night I had to go to the bathroom and I was not allowed to go by myself yet for fear of falling. I waited for some time after calling the receptionist at the front desk. No one came and I had to go so bad that I stood up to go myself. I glanced down at the floor and saw that my drainage tube had fallen out. The nurse came in and as I pointed to the floor, she gasped and said," Oh my goodness!" I jokingly told her that I did not think it was supposed to be on the floor. We both laughed and she left the room to call the doctor that was on call. He told her that we could wait until tomorrow morning before anything could be done for it. Then I was finally able to go to the bathroom.

I wasn't very happy when I heard the news that I would need another drainage tube put in and that I was going back in surgery the next morning.

I love to sing for the Lord, so while the staff and I were in the hallway before my surgery I started singing "This is the day that our Lord has made, let us rejoice and be glad in it." My two nurses started singing with me as they wheeled me into surgery. Then my doctor started singing with us. It was like having a choir in the operating room. It was very special in honor of our Lord.

One morning while I was still in the hospital

recuperating, our daughter Lisa had called frantically. She was beside herself as she had just been told by her gynecologist that her last pap smear came back abnormal and that she was going to need surgery. The doctor thought it might be precancerous. We wanted to wait until I was released from the hospital so I could be there for her.

This is how our Lord works. He does not put on us anything that we can not handle and He will never leave us. I had just found out that I had cancer, now our Lisa had precancerous cells and to top things off, another daughter called with the news that she had cancer. Satan was working overtime, just how much could a family take? But, we knew our Lord was strong enough to give all of us the strength we would need. Neither John nor I were ever afraid because we trusted in Jesus and still do. Besides, He had told me that everything would be fine. While still recuperating in the hospital I was online daily searching for another apartment for John, I and our little Shih Tzu, Beau. One that we would be able to afford.

When we had moved into our current apartment four years earlier, it only took the

Lord six months to have John wind up with the job of groundskeeper for the apartment complex. After six months we were blessed to have our rent adjusted by adding that amount to John's salary and paying zero rent. This was due to the owner's appreciation of the improvements seen on the property by John. Especially in removing heavy vine growth from trees and the landscaping in general. The complex office received new roses and other shrubs. Plus other projects caused the residents to commend the improvements.

But, after three and a half years as the grounds keeper, the property was sold and the staff reduced. No groundskeeper position and no free rent, plus an increase in the current rent, which was beyond our budget.

Everyday someone from our Sunday school class would call and ask me," What are you going to do? Where will you live?" I told them that we were not worried about anything. We were trusting in our Lord for a miracle, and that is exactly what we did.

The complex that we were living in, one of the great things about living there was it had a recreational pool which our grandchildren loved. I can remember Maggie, Erin and Anna jumping into the inner tubes or floating on the raft. We all enjoyed that, but it did not last long since the property was sold. Before the previous owner sold it to them, he had made a clause in the paper work, stating that he wanted both of us to remain there for a month free, in order for us to find a new place, and they agreed to that. This was all in the Lord's plan.

After several days of searching many apartments on the computer, my eyes were getting tired, but our Lord told me to search one more place. So when I was released from the hospital, John and I went to look at it but when we arrived there was a "no vacancy" sign in front of the office. Immediately John wanted to turn around and leave the premises, but The Holy Spirit told me that this was going to be our new home. So I told John what the Holy Spirit had just spoken to me. I told him, "We have to go in."

We knocked on the door of the manager's apartment and they told us to come in, and asked us to sit down. I spoke up and told them that we were interested in a two bedroom and one bathroom apartment on the first floor. The man, who was also the maintenance man, spoke up and told us that he was sorry but he did not have one available. His wife, who is the manager, spoke up and said, "What about the one you are working on?" He told us that it was a mess because it had not been taken care of by the previous resident. He said, we practically had to gut it. I assured him that we definitely were interested in looking at it anyway. He saw that we were not going anywhere, so he finally gave in and let us look at it.

It was about 200 sq. ft. smaller than our other apt. and a wreck, with drywall missing on several walls. Everywhere we looked the paint was in terrible shape, but I felt in my heart that our Lord had planned for this to be our new home. He told us that we would be getting new carpet, kitchen flooring, new stove & dishwasher, but the fridge was okay. Our Lord is so good that when we moved in two months later, the maintenance man added a new fridge also.

We would visit our apartment from time to time to see what progress was taking place. As it started to come to life, it was very nice. But, the bathroom had a very old, small clunky sink, with absolutely no counter top to put anything on it or shelving under it. John and I went to Lowe's and found a beautiful white cabinet with shelves and doors and an extra, large sink. It was so much better than the one we replaced, but it would also become a permanent fixture of the building.

Our family and friends were so happy that we were going to have a nice new place that we could call home. We were never afraid of not being able to find another home, for we trusted in the Lord completely.

This was a miracle that John and I were truly blessed with. We never worried about what was happening in our lives, but it was not always that way. We thought at times we were handing everything over to Him, but like others, because we are human, we were always taking it back. Then the closer we became in our relationship with the Lord, the more we trusted Him with everything. We learned by doing that, it would bring us such peace. Our battles were already won by our Lord when He carried our sins on His cross.

I came home with a drainage tube hanging from my side, it hurt a lot but I knew that this was only a temporary bump in the road. John took such good care of it by checking and emptying it three times a day. He had to be *so very careful while he was emptying it. He would record and measure the fluids. Every time he would clean around it I was leery because I did not want a repeat of what happened at the hospital. The surgery to replace the tube actually hurt more than it did the first time.*

Lisa ended up having her surgery one week after I was released from the hospital. Even though I was still in a lot of pain, I had to be there for her as she was really frightened. I knew that the ride to the hospital was going to be really rough on me because of the gravelly, bumpy roads we had to travel. I used a pillow across my stomach to keep me from hurting more, due to the seat belt pressure.

While we were waiting for her surgery to be completed, I had a chance to play with our granddaughter Remi, she was such a good baby. After the surgery was finished, Lisa's dad and I were brought into a room where her doctor told us that she had gotten it all and that she still believed that it was precancerous. She told us that she sent off some of the cysts to be biopsied. "You should hear the results within a week." Boy, did that sound familiar to me, the part when she said, "I got it all." It reminded me of the time just recently when my oncologist said that he thought my pancreas was precancerous, but later we received the news that it was cancer. I had all of our prayer warriors praying for her.

Lisa and Remi came to stay with us while we each recovered. We were there to help one another. There were still several things that I needed help with that I could not do yet because of my surgery. John stepped in and helped tremendously as he always does. He carried Remi because neither I nor Lisa could do any lifting. She was such a joy to play with. We had a lot of special bonding time.

Taking care of Lisa made my pain lighter, and I treasured every moment of our time together. While she was with us she received the results of her biopsies. It was precancerous and she would not need any treatments. "Praise the Lord."

Our Lord not only gave me the strength for myself, but to also be there for our daughter and precious granddaughter. We had so much fun just being mothers and daughters. She needed my help to get through this, and I was overjoyed that I could do this for her.

When it came time for them to go back home, I was very disheartened. In my thoughts I did not know when I would see them again. They live about two hours away and I could not drive because of my disability, also John was going back to work. But Lisa promised me that it would not be long until we would see each other again, and it was not.

Finally after three weeks had gone by, I went back to see my oncologist, and he told me that the fluid had quit draining enough that he could remove the tube. It was painful for a short time but I was just so relieved to be rid of it.

I healed very nicely from the surgery and you could barely see my scars. Scars are only temporary markings on our body. No matter how bad we think they look, we should not let them steal our joy for the Lord by fretting about them. He looks on the inside of us, at our heart and soul, not the outside.

Our Lord had cured me from my cancer without ever having to take any treatments of any kind. I am so blessed that we found it in time and that the Lord told me that I had cancer. Most people do not find out that they have pancreatic cancer until it is too late and it is usually stage four, then it has already metastasized to other organs.

Our Lord spared my life and had performed another miracle. I believe, that past and present, He wants me to share my testimonies and in doing so I will encourage others and share His good news, and He will receive all the glory.

We Do Believe That Jesus Performs Miracles

John 2:11

11 What Jesus did here in Cana of Galilee was the first of the signs through which he revealed His glory; and his disciples believed in him.

3

Jesus Is Our Hope

Early one day in October of 2015 I woke up to a cool, crispy morning with blustery winds blowing and cooler temperatures which made the beautiful fall leaves descend from the trees. I do not know what your favorite season is, but I love autumn. I love walking through the piles of leaves.

Which reminds me of the time years ago when my two girls were younger, I would gather up all the leaves into a big pile in front of the kids swing set. They would go down the slide and land in the leaves. We would laugh so much, they would say now it is your turn mommy! They would go right back up the slide and go down again. We made so many beautiful memories together that will remain in my heart forever.

I came out of our bedroom to see John, I had no idea of what kind of day I was going to have with my health issues. I tried to speak to him but all my words came out jumbled. I could see the words that I wanted to say, but I was stuttering every word. I just could not make it stop. I felt some numbness on my left side, also my peripheral vision was not good in the left eye. I felt very weak, so weak that I could not walk by myself. John walked me down to our bedroom where I rested for an hour. I got out of the bed because I needed something from the kitchen and as I started to walk down the hall with my walker, my entire body shook uncontrollably like a kangaroo. I was a real mess, but I knew that Jesus is our hope. It kept jerking and before I knew it I was literally hopping down the hall.

By this time John and I both decided that it was time for me to go to the emergency room. When we arrived they brought me to the triage department right away. There I was taken care of by a loving, caring group of doctors and nurses. One of the neurologist that came to see me ordered a cat scan of my brain. I was in so much pain from my fibromyalgia and my chronic pain throughout my entire body that I had a terrible time laying down for the test. I whispered a little prayer to the Lord, "Please help me to be able to lay down and keep still."And that is exactly what He did. I could feel the anxiousness leave my body and I was so calm. I knew in my heart that Jesus was there with me.

After many tests consisting of MRI, Cat scans, Echocardiogram, etc. My results showed that I had suffered a stroke. Never in a million years would I have ever thought that this would happen to me. I looked okay, I just was not acting okay. The neurologist said that the weakness that I was experiencing on my left side and the blurred peripheral vision were caused from the stroke. The stuttering and the hopping were not. The doctors had no idea of what was going on with me or what they should do next. They had never seen this kind of behavior before.

The funny thing is that I had been trying to see a neurologist for several months and now I had four of them working on my case. Going through the emergency at the hospital is the fastest way to see a specialist that you need, even though it may be a long wait. I remained in the hospital a few days, but while I was there my heart went into A-fib twice. A couple doctors said that they *thought I had A-fib but the other two were not sure. I had to have a heart monitor implanted in my chest wall. I was told that as long as I did not have any episodes that the doctor would remove it in a year.*

At this time the neurologist that was in charge of my case from the hospital referred me to see another neurologist who specialized in people that have had a stroke. This doctor also agreed that my other symptoms, the hopping and stuttering were not caused by the stroke and she referred me to see another neurologist who, I found out, was in charge of a Functional Movement Disorder clinic where they try to retrain your brain. So, I am now hopping through doctors as well as hopping down the hall.

At my first visit, she had me do all sorts of things, like walking down the hall to check my gait and balance. Both of my feet were dragging as I walked with my cane. She had me do several eye and hand coordination exercises. I felt like I was back in preschool. While I was doing these things she video taped everything. When I was finished with everything, she told both John and I that she thought I was experiencing a Functional Movement Disorder. Neither one of us had ever heard of this. She explained it like this; Parkinson's disease is that the brain cells hardware can not be cured, but what I have is a software problem, where the connection of the brain cells are there but they are not connecting properly. I have a good chance of being cured, but people with Parkinson's do not. She said that she was going to show the video to the doctor in charge of the Functional Movement Disorder clinic to see if I would qualify for the specialized rehab clinic. Finally we felt like we had hope from the doctor's, but John and I received our hope from the Lord.

We had one more visit before I was accepted. I talked to a Psychologist, and an Occupational and Physical therapist, and found out about the program and how it works. Before we left, I told the doctor in charge that my disability case was coming up soon and that I had been waiting for 2 ½ years for it to be heard. We agreed that we would wait till after my hearing, it was only a few weeks away. She explained to me that once I was in the program that I would not be able to leave there for a week. This program was extremely hard to get into. They only accept one a week but I knew that the Lord was in charge and He was taking care of me.

My prayer warriors, let me share with you that I had been praying for awhile that it would be His will that I would not have to go to court for the hearing, and my lawyer would call me with the news that the judge had already granted me my total disability. So a week before my hearing he called to tell me that all of our prayers had been answered. I would not have to go to court. Is not our Lord amazing? Once again it was His perfect timing. He knew that John and I would really need the money and John could finally retire for good. Working those long hours were really getting to him and his surgically repaired back.

I never wanted to put a label on myself for being disabled, in fact it took me 1 ½ years to file my disability claim. I just did not want to admit it. Giving up my career of thirty five years of being a Certified Nursing Assistant and an Activity Director for part of that time really cut to the core of me, it hurt deep inside of my heart and I cried for weeks. I can not explain how much I cared for my patients, they entrusted their recovery to me and these beautiful people were family to me. I was told by so many of the family members that they loved me and the manner in which I cared for their loved ones. Oh how I miss them even to this very day. Having to give this up did not sit very well with me. Our Lord really had to comfort me in this storm because I was not handling it at all.

A week before I was to be admitted to the clinic, one of the nurses called to say that they had just had a last minute cancellation. She said, "What a coincidence that this should happen!" I told her that this was not a coincidence, but a blessing from the Lord.

John and I arrived on a Sunday afternoon. We were greeted with such anticipation and they made us feel right at home. I came in with a positive attitude determined to get better. Once we were settled in, they took a video of me prior to the treatments. They wanted to record my hopping down the hall, stuttering, tremors and dragging my feet. I came in using a cane that I had been using for several years. On the third day of my treatments, my physical therapist took away my cane, which was my safety net, and wanted me to walk down the hall. I did not think I could do it. She told me to repeat these words;"

Heel toe, Heel toe", she was basically teaching me how to walk all over again.

My days there consisted of very vigorous, different kinds of therapies. I was totally exhausted by the end of each day. I would start off with physical therapy, which was the start of being able to walk again. During physical therapy she wanted me to walk up the stairs, but I was so frightened that I gripped the railing and froze. I eventually gave in because I was determined to get well, so I put one foot in front of the other and slowly shuffled up the stairway. She asked if she could clock me as I climbed the stairs. At first it took twenty two seconds to ascend the stairs, and by the end of the week I was going up in just seven seconds. Going up the stairs was much easier than going down which petrified me. I would stand at the top of the stairs and become so frightened at the thought of falling down them and really getting hurt

She also worked on my balance since my gait was really off. I walked the balance beams and around the track. They could not believe how well I was doing and neither could I, but I knew it was from the Lord. My occupational therapist also worked on my balance and my strength. She would toss me a balloon and I had to keep hitting it back to her using both hands. I was moving all around back and forth, sideways and I had not done that in a very long time. Then I would go to speech therapy where she would make me read things out loud and showed me pictures of different situations and I had to tell her what I thought and what I would do in that situation. After lunch I would start it all over again. I would round up each day with my psychologist, where she would talk to me about the day. I would listen to very relaxing music with sounds of the rain forest and ocean waves while answering her questions. A couple of times I would drift off to sleep because I was so wiped out from the strenuous activities during the day. When the rehab was completed, I felt such a great sense of accomplishment and praised the Lord.

This program seemed to help some, or so we thought but as soon as I came home I started stuttering again but not quite as bad as before. My body still shook uncontrollably and still does. I will have jerks every now and then like I am having a seizure. The only way I can stop them is if someone holds me and tells me that everything is okay. It is not very often that I could help myself come out of one. John has helped me through most of them by holding me as he calms me. He always tells me that he loves me, that I can do this and that everything will be alright.

I called my neurologist to let her know what was going on, that these Non- Epileptic Seizures were back and they were more vigorous and coming closer together. She told me that she was sorry but unfortunately the program was not 100%. I would keep bouncing back and forth with them. Unfortunately there is no medication for these either(or so they thought, as you will see later).

A Non-Epileptic Seizure (Functional Movement Disorder) is when they resemble epileptic seizures on the outside, even though their causes are different. The FMD seizures are characterized by episodic disturbances of normal function and control that superficially resemble epileptic attacks. But they are not caused by epileptic activity in the brain and are thought to have a psychological basis usually caused by depression and trauma events in one's life. I needed to try to retrain my brain every day by meditating, and reading out loud for the stuttering, at least I do not stutter very often now. I need to incorporate more physical and occupational therapy into my daily activities. I tried to do the exercises, but I hurt so bad from my chronic pain and fibromyalgia that makes me burn literally from my head to my toes. Still, I do them because I want to get better. I know eventually they may be able to help me.

These attacks are trying to keep me from doing my daily activities. But, if someone asks me if they can take me to lunch, I tell them yes because these attacks are not going to stop me from having fun. I usually end up having one in the restaurant that could end up with me sliding out of the chair, which is quite embarrassing to me. I know that I should not be embarrassed, but I am. I am not going to let them rule me, if I stay at home and do not go to my outings, then they will. I joined a chronic pain meeting where we meet once a month and a cancer support meeting also once a month. We have a great group that listens to each other's problems. They share with the group different ways that they have used to cope with their own sickness and pain. It is very beneficial to me.

Since I never know when an attack may occur,

I will not jeopardize someones life or my own. My doctor's have told me not to drive, so I have stopped driving for awhile. This has made me feel depressed, but I cannot let this take away my joy for the Lord, so I have learned to accept this. I feel like my license has been revoked and I have lost part of my independence. At least I felt this way in the past, now I just pray about it and ask the Lord to help me to not feel this way. I think the hardest thing about my health situations is not being able to drive, since I cannot go see our grandchildren like I used to. Both of my daughter's live two hours away. I used to get in my car and drive wherever I needed to go. I drove for thirty five years. If a friend of mine needed me for anything, I was there for them.

Six years ago after taking many hours of various kinds of vigorous therapies, I was finally able to get out of the wheelchair and drive around eighteen miles before I would have to pull over and let John take over. If I drove any further than that, I would be screaming from horrible pain in my legs. There were times that I was not sure how I would make it home because I was in so much pain. It had taken 2 ½ years to be able to drive that far of a distance, and now it has been two years since I have driven at all. Not being able to drive has developed into a different type of deep inner pain with tears.

But, I am not giving up on my Jesus, He is my hope that I cling to. Our Lord has showed me countless times that through my pain, I can still have joy. I now walk around with a smile on my face for Him. His Spirit has reminded me that if I do not use these smiling dimples, then no one is going to believe that I trust in Him completely. He is my hope and He can be yours too if only you call out His name, accept Him as your Savior and repent of your sins.

We Do Believe That Jesus Is Our Hope

Colossians 1:27

27 To them God has chosen to make known among the Gentiles the glorious riches of this mystery, which is Christ in you, the hope of glory.

1 Corinthians 15:19a

If only for this life we have hope in Christ.

4

Jesus Is The Prince Of Peace

In July of 2018, I had another six month follow up with my oncologist that had performed surgery on my pancreas and the removal of my spleen, and was scheduled for a CT scan on my chest, abdomen and pelvic area. As I was laying on the frigid ice cold table, while waiting for the test to begin, the nurse was trying to put in an IV in any vein that she could find. She had to use a big gauge needle, that way when she ran the thick contrast dye through my veins the doctor would be able to see what he was looking for. She tried to do it twice, then another nurse tried twice, without any luck. She left the room to find a certain tech that had been known to find the patients veins fairly easy. He came into the room and looked at my veins and told me that my veins like to roll and that made it harder to stick me. He checked my small veins by making me squeeze a ball as he was putting the band close to the area of the vein that he had been frantically looking for. He finally found one that he was sure would work, he stuck me one time and the line went through perfectly. I told him that while the nurse was trying to find him in the hall I was praying for him to be able to get it right on the first try. I was already in a lot of pain and I definitely did not need anymore. He thanked me for my prayers. "Praise the Lord", the results were negative.

WEDDING DAY FEB 12, 2005

JOHN & CINDY ORIOL

VOWS RENEWAL FEB 12, 2015

JOHN & CINDY ORIOL

DAUGHTER SUZANNE & FAMILY

AIRIANNA, SUZANNE, JEFF & ZACHARIA

DAUGHTER JULIE & FAMILY

ERIN, JAMIE, MAGGIE & JULIE

DAUGHTER NICOLE & FAMILY

KATIE, NICOLE & PAT

MARLA (CISSY) ABELL

DAUGHTER LISA & FAMILY

LISA & REMIAH

DAUGHTER MICHELLE & FAMILY

NICK, ZOEY, MICHELLE & HUNTER

I believe that every one of us at one time or another have had a certain part of our body that we liked best. It could be your eyes, legs, waistline, hair etc.

Mine Is The Breast

As a child at the age of ten, several of my girl friends were already blossoming into a teenager but I hadn't yet. I was a late bloomer.

When I was growing up between the ages of thirteen-sixteen, girls and boys were brutal with their words. I was really thin, pale and very tall, so they called me ugly names like stretch, bean pole, giraffe, and a white albino. I used to get beaten up on the way home from school. Those horrible names hurt me so bad that I did not have any self-esteem about myself. I carried this all through my adolescent years and later into my adult years, until I met Jesus. He showed me that I was fearfully and wonderfully made.

Jesus, a man that does not look at our outward appearances. He only cares what is in our hearts. Jesus, himself was ridiculed, beaten, and called slanderous names.

December16, 2017 I went for my yearly

mammogram. I was truly dreading it because in the past they had always hurt me. Before the test I said a prayer, "Lord, I know that you are with me. Please do not let this hurt too much." I also prayed that if there was anything suspicious that the doctor would find it. My prayers were answered.

After I was finished getting the mammogram my technician went to show the doctor my results. She came back in the room to tell me that I was going to need an ultrasound. After the ultrasound was completed the doctor came in and showed me on the ultrasound his findings. I had two small cysts on top of each other like a snowman, in my right breast. He told me that they were benign and that he had seen this happen before in other female patients. He said they were filled with fluid and that I would not have to come back until my yearly checkup. I told him that I did not want to wait a year, I said that I wanted to be rechecked in six months, but he insisted upon a year. He told me not to worry.

I assured him that I was not worried. I told him that I will put this in our Lord's hands and keep it there. And that is just what I did. Jesus gave both John and I so much peace.

On July 19, John had to have his left hand operated on because his left thumb joint did not have any cartilage left and it was bone on bone. His ring finger tendon would not slide through its sheath causing a "Trigger Finger condition". This was all so painful for him.

Cissy brought us to the hospital because I still could not drive. She would come back later to take me to lunch with her grandson. We went to a park, not too far from the hospital. We had so much fun watching him run around. He was so funny he would go under the swings and act like he was fixing them so no one would get hurt. He loved playing with my cane, acting like he was hurt. We had a wonderful lunch from Mc'Donalds. I love to order the chicken nuggets happy meal that way I get everything with it, the nuggets, fries and a drink. We always have a great time every time we are together. When she took me back to the hospital John was still in surgery so she left to run errands and I was told to call her when he was in recovery. I waited in the waiting room with anticipation of seeing my John. I could not wait to see him and tell him I love him.

While waiting I looked across the room and

there was a woman who looked very troubled. She had been crying and looked very nervous. She was really shaking. I am ashamed to tell you all that I just turned my head and started reading my book that I had brought with me. I heard the Holy Spirit say," I want you to go and talk with her." I said," Are you sure? I do not think I can." He told me that I could with His help, and His words would be my words. He told me that I could help her to feel better with His help. I hesitated for a moment and then I got out of my chair and went to where she was sitting. I asked her if it would be okay if I sat down with her. She told me that she did not mind. I asked how she was doing. She told me that she was not doing well at all. She said," I want to kill myself." I asked her why and she told me that there were so many hurtful things going on in her life. I asked her if she wanted to talk about it. Without divulging any of her information she really needed help that day. I asked the Lord's Spirit what I could do to help her. He wanted me to give her the book that I had brought with me to read, while John was in surgery. It just happened to be my first book titled "IF ONLY" that the Lord and I had written together. He told me that He wanted me to read the back of the cover to her it reads, "When your life seems to be falling apart hold tight to Jesus." He wanted me to tell her that I cared about her and that I was there for her. Then He told me to embrace her in my arms and start praying. I said," I do not know what to say." So through the Holy Spirit's inspiration I prayed,"Let the binds of Satan disappear from this precious woman completely. Give her peace and comfort, the kind that only comes from you." I asked Him to open her heart so she could tell her children what was going on in her mind and that she needed their help. After the prayer I started talking to her about the Lord. I wanted to see if she was a believer. She like I, at one time did not know that a believer could have a personal relationship with Jesus. She was completely fascinated about that.

We talked for quite a while about Him. Then I asked her how she felt now and if she still wanted to commit suicide. She told me that she no longer wanted to. She said" I now know that I have someone who truly cares and His name is Jesus." I reminded her that if she did commit suicide that she would be completely out of the picture but she would be leaving a big hole in her children's lives. She started crying and thanked me over and over again. I told her that it is not me. It's Him using me as a vessel. What a beautiful privilege to be used by our Lord.

Not only had I come to the hospital for John's surgery but I was also there to help save a woman's life from Satan- The father of all lies but I never could have done it without my Lord's Holy Spirit that dwells inside of me. I was there to help her see that "Nothing" could ever be so bad to take one's own life. Cry out to Jesus because He cares, He will hear your cry and rescue you. If I had not been there and listened to His call and obeyed Him, I would have missed out on a miraculous miracle. I saw the Prince of peace throughout those precious moments when He was healing her heart and letting her know that He cares for her. Together with the Holy Spirit we were able to bring this child of God closer to His son Jesus. This is another one of His precious miracles I hold deeply within my heart. When we ask Him for His peace we will receive it.

John's hand surgery went well. I could not wait for him to wake up in recovery for two reasons. The first one was I wanted to see and talk to my love and we could go home together. And secondly I wanted to share with him about the amazing journey that the Lord had taken me on earlier that day . It was an amazing experience being used by the Lord's Spirit.

Wow it just goes to show you that The Lord can and will use anyone of us as a vessel to complete His mission as long as we allow ourselves to be used and obey His will. The keywords, "Obey His will,"are what we need to do and then honor Him with glory and praise. We just need to adjust our schedules to meet with Him.

We Do Believe That Jesus Is The Prince of Peace

Isaiah 9:6

6 For unto us a child is born, to us a son is given, and the government will be on his shoulders. And he will be called Wonderful Counselor, Mighty God, Ever lasting Father, Prince of Peace.

5

Jesus Is Love

In July of 2018, I had my six month follow up with my oncologist that had performed the surgery on my pancreas and the removal of my spleen. I was scheduled for a CT scan on my chest, abdomen and pelvic area.

As I was laying on that frigid, ice cold table while waiting for the test to begin, the nurse looked over both of my arms and hands to find a good vein that would work when she would run the thick contrast dye through it. She thought she finally found one as she administered a large gauge needle in my vein but it rolled making it impossible to use it. She decided that she was going to try one more time, same as before it did not work. By this time I was really hurting from the needles plus the burning of my chronic pain and fibromyalgia. I really hurt when I lay on those tables. She left the room in order to find a tech who was well known to be able to stick people one try. He administered the tight rubber band around my arm and he was able to retrieve blood for my labs. I told him that while I was waiting I was in here praying for him. He thanked me.

Now we were ready to get the ball rolling. I was still very cold. That room probably had ice cold temperatures like they have in the morgue. The tech gave me two warm blankets, finally I felt warmer. She was almost finished with the test, but now it was time for the contrast dye to flow through my body. If you have not ever had it done to you, there's a metallic taste in your mouth and then you feel this hot sensation going through your entire body. It makes you believe that you have wet yourself. In fact when the test was finished I was praying that had not happened.

Immediately John and I went upstairs to my oncologist office to receive the results, I love how you can get the results back so quickly. After going over them, he came into the room where John and I were waiting patiently for favorable results. He told us that he did not see any signs of cancer anywhere. We all looked at each other and I said, "Praise the Lord."

The Holy Spirit told me to ask him if I should be concerned about having two small cysts in my right breast. He said, "Yes, you should definitely be concerned. That is how we found your pancreatic cancer from two cysts." Then he told me that he knew of a great breast surgeon who came highly recommended, and would have them get in touch with me.

Our first visit with the specialist was on August 8. When we walked into his office we were greeted with such joy that we felt right at home. I was brought into a room and I was told to strip down to my waist. By this time I had so many different doctors examining me. I honestly felt as if I was on the show "Candid Camera," Smile, you are on the set of Candid Camera." Oh well, it was just one more doctor examining me.

The doctor came into the room, shook our hands and explained how the examination would proceed. He checked both breasts and then left the room to look over my mammogram findings. He came back in to tell me that he honestly did not *think that there was anything to be concerned about. But just to be on the safe side he ordered another mammogram and ultrasound to be sure of the mammograms findings.*

On August 21, I had both tests repeated as before. The mammogram hurt really bad, I could not wait for it to be over. During the ultrasound as I was looking at the pictures I saw where my two small cysts had now became a cluster and there were finger like markings spreading away from the breast into the breast tissue.

Here was the cancer that the Lord had spoken to me about, but He had already told me that everything was going to be fine. Only He and I knew until then. If I had not listened to the Holy Spirit about me having cancer again and gotten the doctor's attention when I did "Having Joy In The Midst Of The Storm" would not have been written because I would not be here. I was not afraid at all about any of this because Jesus is love and I knew that He was cradling me in His loving arms. Because of the new findings, the doctor said that she was going to biopsy the cysts right away. I knew I had to go to the waiting room where John was anticipating my arrival to go home with him. I explained everything to him and I asked him to start praying. I had been told in the past that biopsies were quite painful.

I had been taking blood thinners for a while now due to the stroke that I had in the past. But because I had not been off of them for seven days, the biopsy gave me a very large and painful hematoma. It was so horrible to look at and very painful. Neither I nor the nurses had ever seen anything like this. They were all very concerned on how they were going to stop the bleeding.

I can not begin to tell you how intense the pain was. I had never felt such pain, it was such a horrifying experience. I was looking at the hematoma and the colors changed from black to blue, mostly black. By this time I had asked for the nurse to go and get John. I needed him to hold my hand because the nurse had just spoken to me that she could not let me leave like that and she was going to have to press down really hard on the hematoma to make the blood clot. She stretched her body over mine and pressed down with all the strength she had for an hour. I believe with all my heart that Jesus was there with me because there is no way that I could have gotten through that, it was horribly traumatic.

I was squirming all over that table just

begging her to quit but she said that she could not let up on the pressure, that she had to make it clot. When John was holding my hand to try to comfort me, I cried out to Jesus,"Please lessen this pain." He immediately opened His arms as I entered in them. He held me ever so gently, whispering in my ear,"I love you and together we will get through this."Between Him holding me, and John holding my hand while telling me he loved me and lots of shedding of all our tears, I made it through that horrible ordeal.

The nurse kept apologizing over and over again. She, like us, could not believe that the mammogram doctor did not wait until my blood thinner pills were out of my system before taking a biopsy. It was finally time to go home and I could not wait to get out of there and go to the comforts of our home. I wanted a quiet place so I could cry as loud as I wanted to and that is just what I did. I cried so hard because I had been traumatized by that whole procedure. I live with chronic pain in my entire body but that pain I could not stop. I had to use ice packs constantly to keep the swelling down.

Two days later my phone rang, I picked it up and on the other end was the doctor who had done the biopsy on me. She asked me how I was feeling and I told her that I was hurting really bad from the hematoma. She apologized to me again and then proceeded to tell me that she had some bad news to tell me, that the biopsy had come back showing cancer, it was a triple negative three carcinoma, that means my hormones were not involved. The cancer had started in the ducts of the milk glands, but had already infiltrated into the breast tissues. These were the fingers I had seen during my previous ultrasound. She said that it was very aggressive, on a grade level with one of being not aggressive and grade three being the worst, mine was a three. She then told me that this needed to be taken care of very soon. She asked me how I felt about the results that she had just read to me(really?). I said," Can I tell you a secret? I already knew because the Lord had already told me when I asked Him." She told me that my faith is what would get me through all of this, and that she would be praying for me. As we were finishing up our conversation, I told her to have a blessed day and then I pushed the end button on my cell phone.

I sat there starring at the phone and the scriptures that were hanging on the wall in my *prayer room where the Lord and I commune together. I asked the Lord to give me the strength that I would need for the months ahead. I told Him that I loved Him and thanked Him for the love and peace I was already feeling.*

As I was contemplating about what she had just told me, a name popped in my thoughts and I remembered that the only relative I had with breast cancer was a cousin on my mom's side of the family. Sadly she had succumbed to her battle many years ago.

John had been out earlier in the morning running a few errands. I could not wait for him to come back home so that I could tell him the news. I needed his strong and loving arms around me as I cry in them, and knew that everything was going to fine because my Lord was really all I needed in any crisis. My prayer was for Him to allow me to be able to tell my two daughters, Lisa & Michelle, the results at the same time. Well He did just that. I tried to call Lisa first because I thought Michelle was working. You know how you want to share good or bad news with somebody and the phone is always busy or the person you are trying to reach is not at home. Well, this was the case with me. I called Michelle and her phone was also busy. I thought out loud that I hope they are talking to each other. I kept dialing both of their numbers several times but it was always busy. Finally they called me. They had been talking to each other and when they saw how many times I had been trying to get a hold of them they knew that it was pretty serious, and needed them both. I said that my results from the biopsies came back and it was cancer. You could hear a pin drop, there was a long pause as silence filled the room. I waited patiently for one of them to speak first, finally Michelle spoke up and said, "Everything is going to be fine, mom, and we will all be okay." I could hear the fear in their voices. They were shocked and feeling numb, and I told them that this was going into the hands of Jesus, where I completely believed that He would take care of me, and said to them, "Do not be afraid."

To hear that someone you love, especially your own mother, has cancer and that she is going to have to take chemo is really hard to comprehend. It brought back sad memories of the day when my mother told my family that she had esophageal cancer and that she herself was going to have chemotherapy treatments.

I asked both of them if they were okay. They assured me that they were and proceeded to tell me that they loved me.

John arrived home and came into my prayer room where I had just received the news about my cancer. As I was holding the hands of my soulmate, and starring at his beautiful, blue eyes I proceeded to tell him, that I was diagnosed with having breast cancer. He squeezed my hands, while letting out a big sigh and tears trickling down his cheeks, he told me he loved me and we were going to keep trusting in the Lord to give us His healing love, power and strength.

I want to share this with you, my readers, that day I became stronger than I have ever felt before. If any of you have ever seen the movie "The Grinch Who Stole Christmas," at the very end of the movie his heart grew three sizes the size of his small heart and he felt so strong and at peace. That is the same feeling I was experiencing from the Lord. I knew that as long as I clung to Him I would get through this. He gave me so much strength that day and the days to follow. He has taught me to be still and wait upon Him. I may not like His ways of answering my prayers but He truly knows what is best for me. His Spirit reminds me that I have to be patient and rely on Him for everything. I will continue to give Him all the glory, honor and praise that He alone deserves.

I will encourage others to put their trust in Him completely, they might be going through a hard trial also. Some times their crisis is what I have just been through, or possibly even worse. Looking to the Lord to help you to overcome whatever Satan throws in your way takes the courage that is only available from Jesus.

I felt in my heart that I needed to go see our girls to make sure that they were okay. I did not like having them finding out about my cancer on the phone and besides I really needed to feel their arms around me. A friend of mine, Carol, brought me up there. Michelle was cooking us chili for dinner and was just starting it when we arrived. Carol decided she was going to take over in making the chili, so Michelle, Lisa and I could spend time going over the results of my biopsy.

As they were studying them I tried to explain to them the same way it was explained to me. The medical terminology was really hard to read, but we finally made sense of it. The cancer was *very aggressive and had already traveled into the breast tissues, and was very serious. We hugged each other as the tears rolled down our cheeks. I reiterated to the both of them that if they needed to talk about the cancer, I was there for them.*

As we started down the hall we could smell the delicious aromas of the chili. Hunter told us that supper was ready. It was delicious, but I really wanted to taste Michelle's chili that she had wanted to cook for us but by Carol making it, that gave my daughters and I time to express any emotions that we had bottled up inside. It was a wonderful time visiting with my beautiful grandchildren. It is so hard on me every time I visit them, not knowing when I will see them again because of the long distance between us. With Hunter's sports, Michelle being a supervisor at UPS, plus Lisa studying online to become a medical technologist, it's hard for us to get together especially since I can not drive.

Carol and I had already decided that before we went back home, we would visit my friend Betty and her family since she lived close to Michelle. She insisted that we stay for two nights. We had a wonderful time with her, reminiscing about things that her and I had done in the past. We used to love singing together, especially Loretta Lynn's songs. When it came time for us to leave on our journey back home, we hugged each other goodbye, as tears rolled down our cheeks. We are like sisters that have always been so close to each other, no matter the distance.

On August 29, John took me to see my breast surgeon. The very first words that he said to us was that he was so sorry that he had misdiagnosed me in agreeing with the other doctor while going over my old mammogram results. I thank the Lord that he had ordered another mammogram and ultrasound just to be on the safe side at my first visit. I told him," Thank you for being so thorough, if you had not been we would not have caught it in time and you & I might not be having this conversation."

Now it was time for him to see my grossly, enlarged hematoma that was the color of an egg plant, a dark purple that almost looked black. He took one hard long look at it and said,"Oh my, Cindy! they should have never done this to you while you were still on the blood thinners. They should have waited for them to be completely out of your system, it usually takes around seven days." He regretfully told us that he could not *operate on me until it had shrunk significantly. He said that I would be in horrible pain in the breast area for the rest of my life if he had done it, but he would not do that to me.*

Not only was my doctor feeling discouraged about everything, John and I were also. Here I was standing there, knowing that this was very serious, that the cancer was growing rapidly and I knew that it had to be done as soon as possible, but there was not anything he could do for me. The waiting time would be prolonged but as in every situation, John and I trusted in the Lord, He is love. I went home and called several of my prayer warriors to pray specifically that my hematoma would start shrinking and disappear quickly. I have never had anything to hurt me so badly before, except for the time I was in the wheelchair for almost a year and I could only keep my legs straight out, or I would scream in excruciating pain. I was down on my knees praying to our Lord to take away this horrible pain from the hemotoma and asked Him to please make it disappear soon so that I could have the surgery. I could not even let John hug me. The Lord answered my prayers and the prayers of my prayer warriors as it started shrinking more each day. I still continued to wear the ice packs, daily. You talk about being cold, but I had to do it so the hematoma would shrink.

A few of my friends and family members had asked me what did the pain feel like? I told them that it was one of the most painful experiences that I have ever felt. They felt really sorry for me.

I was scheduled for another mammogram on the left breast to make sure there were not any cysts in it. This took place in the earlier days of September. I was really dreading this for fear of them touching my hematoma in any way, so before I let them begin the test, I told them if they were going to be close to my hematoma to please be very careful. They said that they would not go anywhere near it. The test was finally finished and now I would just have to wait to talk to the doctor. If I did not know Jesus I would have been really scared. "Praise the Lord," everything turned out great. Jesus is Love, and He made sure that the breast was not touched in any way, no pain!

On September 12, I had another appointment with my surgeon to see if the hematoma had gone down enough so that I would be able to have my surgery I so desperately needed. He measured it and made ink markings for him to use as a gauge to see if it shrank more. He then told us it had begun to shrink but not enough for surgery, and he was so discouraged. Because the cancer was so aggressive, he was wanting to operate as soon as possible. He asked me if I had a chemo specialist in mind yet. I told him, "No, but I really want to stay with the same group of doctors that you are with." He then suggested someone in his building.

On September 15, not only was it our daughter Lisa's birthday, but it was the day I met the most amazing chemotherapy doctor. Her staff was so kind to both John and I. We felt loved and at peace immediately. She told me that I was definitely going to have to take chemo therapy but that I would not need radiation. I was stilling praying to the Lord that I would not have to, but Jesus knows what is best for me. I will be honest with you I was not happy at all about taking it. Ever since I watched my own mother become so sick with each chemo treatment she took for her esophageal cancer, which made her appetite for food diminish and she became so weak. This hurts me to say it, my mother lost her battle with cancer, but heaven gained another angel when Jesus took her home. Please excuse me while I get a tissue, because every time I think of her and my dad, I cry. Dad lost his life several years earlier from a massive heart attack. I was always one of those people that had told everyone that I would never take chemo therapy and I meant it with all my heart. I did not want to suffer as mom had. Her quality of life was limited and she was so sick that she could not enjoy life with her family and friends. Crying out to the Lord I asked Him," What should I do Lord?" I had my answer within a total of five minutes. He had also reassured me that everything was going to be fine.

So when the breast surgeon asked me what I had decided to do, I told him I wanted a double mastectomy and I did not want to have any reconstruction done even though the other one was cancer free. Since we talked about how aggressive it was, I was not going to take the chance of maybe having it come back in six months and have to operate on the other one. It had already spread out of the breast milk ducts and was filtering into the breast tissue. He immediately agreed with me and told me I had made a wise decision.

But a few people that I know got really upset because I chose to do it that way. I told them that I appreciated their concerns, but this is what the Lord wanted me to do, besides John and I felt at peace with our decision.

On September 25, I had to have my preadmission testing done to make sure I was healthy enough to have surgery, and I was. My hematoma had finally shrunk enough to have the operation. So on October 3, I said goodbye to my favorite part of my body, but as I really pondered over that, I now believe my favorite part is my heart and soul because Jesus's Spirit resides there. I felt so good in my clothes and with my shape and now it was being taken away from me, but that was just only vanity, wasn't it?

My surgery lasted for three hours and then I spent another hour in the recovery room. When I woke up and saw my precious John starring down at me, with tears trickling down his face while he was holding my hand, I cried. I was so happy to see him. My tears flowed out like a waterfall and I knew that I was okay, besides the Lord had already reassured me that I would be.

The kind nurses wheeled me up to my room. About an hour had passed and Cissy arrived at the hospital to relieve John so he could go home. He was really exhausted, he had been there all day and also our dog, Beau needed to go out. But John would not have had it any other way. He wanted to stay with me, but after talking to him he reluctantly gave in and went home.

Cissy and I talked for awhile, but I was still very groggy from the anesthesia. I could barely mumble a few words so she did most of the talking. While she was carrying on a conversation she glanced my way and happened to see that I was having a very hard time breathing. I was gasping for air and clutching at my chest. I was also experiencing some pain and heaviness in my chest around my heart. She ran out of the room hollering for someone to come quickly. She screamed," I think she might be having a heart attack."

The nurse came in almost immediately with an EKG machine. She attached icy, cold leads on me to record the tests. After showing the results to the doctor, he came to the conclusion that it was not a heart attack but was a panic attack instead, which mimics the same symptoms as having a heart attack. I was having shortness of breath, chest heaviness, and pain on the left side. *Unfortunately I had experienced them in the past, when I had my second nervous break down and was so deeply depressed. But with the doctors(and the Lord's) help, I had gotten better.*

Cissy left reluctantly, because she was afraid I might have another attack. But I assured her that I was in great hands. Settling down for the night, I felt the presence of the Lord, so I wasn't alone. I noticed that my gown had slid to the side a little, and thought to myself," Do I dare look at it while John is gone?" I decided that I was brave enough, besides I had the Lord with me.

I looked down and staring back at me was this horrible looking, sunken-in chest. It looked like I had been ran over by a semi truck. It was all black and blue, mostly black and had a grin(like the Grinch) from side to side where the doctor had performed the surgery. I gasped, began to cry, I thought it would have had bandages on it, but it did not. I was not ready to see it and now I wished that I had waited for John to be there with me.

Before the surgery I had gone on the internet to see what a woman would look like after having a double mastectomy. Nothing- I mean nothing could have prepared me for what my eyes were looking upon. It was such a ghastly sight, and so overwhelming.

As I was crying buckets of tears, I asked the Lord to hold me, I just needed to feel the comfort and warmth of His embrace. Just to be held by the rock I cling to. He is Love, and He reminded me that I am fearfully and wonderfully made. I began to thank Him for never leaving my side and for allowing me to be able to spend more quality time with my family and friends. I put my trust in Him completely, the one who promises me that He is my rock I cling to as I travel through the fierce storms.

I remained in the hospital for four days. The staff were very good to both John and I. We had revival every day in my room, for those of you who know me I can never stop talking enough about our Lord and what He has done in my life and will do in theirs.

On the last day I was preparing to go home, but before I left I wanted to take a shower to refresh my body, then I would not have to take one when I went home that day. While my male nurse was preparing my shower I told him that because of my scar I had a new nickname for myself, I said, I am the "Grinch Who Stole

Christmas." He said, "There was no way I could be called that. You are the nicest woman I have ever met." He said to me, "I just love you, you are such a special woman." He was a very nice, young man who just happened to know the Lord. We had wonderful conversations about our precious Lord and Savior.

I finished with my very, hot shower where the water just ran down my back and made me feel so good and refreshed, then I put on clean clothes. It was the first time I had any of my clothes on since the surgery. It felt so good wearing them instead of those cold gowns with short sleeves and the open back. As I was putting my shirt on I noticed that it was too big. It did not fit my body at all and was not very flattering which caused a sadness to come over me, but only for a moment. I recalled my conversation with the Lord earlier where He told me I was beautiful so the sadness disappeared.

I came home with two drainage tubes hanging from one side of the chest to the other." Oh no! Here we go again." I was so scared to let John empty them for fear of what happened before when my drainage tube had fallen out after my pancreatic cancer surgery. He was so gentle as he cleaned each tube and emptied them. Once again he had to measure the quantity from each tube and record it's findings. I was so grateful on the day they were taken out. It was painful but not as much as the surgery would be to replace them.

At my post-op visit the doctor told us that everything was healing very nicely. That nasty looking hematoma was gone, and I would not have to deal with that pain anymore. He had also removed the heart monitor implant since I had gone a year without any episodes. Before we left his office I told him that John had a question that he wanted to ask him. So very seriously John said," Doctor, when will they grow back?" With a sorrowful face and fighting off his tears this sensitive, caring doctor said," I am so sorry, but they won't. John, while laughing, told him that it was a joke. I laughed so hard that I nearly fell off the table. Then he joined in the laughter.

We Do Believe That Jesus Is Love

Psalms 86:13 "For great is your love to me; you have delivered me from the depths of the grave."

Ephesians 3: 17-19 "So that Christ may dwell in your hearts through faith. And I pray that you, being rooted and established in love, may have power together with all the saints to grasp how wide and long and high and deep is the love of Christ and to know this love that surpasses knowledge, that you may be filled to the measure of all fullness of God."

6

Jesus Is The Light

On October 20, John took me to see the chemo specialist. There had been several weeks from our first appointment with her until now, she examined me and was very happy with the results. She told me that my breast surgeon would have to insert a port under my skin. This would be very helpful while I was taking the chemo. She made me an appointment for a day of training to learn about the port, how it works and how to take care of it.

They insert the port usually in the chest, and the attached tube goes into a vein near the heart, then a catheter connects the port to a vein under the skin. The port has a spectrum through which the medicine can be injected and blood samples can be drawn many times.

My port was surgically inserted on October 30, but before the surgery, a friend of mine from church had given me some pennies with crosses cut out of each one of them and told me that at every appointment and new people that I would meet, I should give them a penny in Jesus name and tell them that I had already covered them in prayers. So I brought them with me that day and was prepared for how the Holy Spirit was going to be seen everywhere, and I was excited to once again talk about our Lord and what an amazing Savior He is.

A nurse came in to get my vital signs and I gave him the first penny. He was so surprised when I said, "I give you this penny in Jesus name," he kept repeating the words, "Thank You." When he stepped out of the room, I could hear him at the front desk telling the other nurses and doctors about what had just happened, as he was showing it to all of them.

One by one they came in asking for their penny. They were all so excited to receive it and to know that through the Holy Spirit I had prayed for them. I told them that I give all the glory, honor and praise to the Lord. When my surgeon came in to talk to me, right before I was being wheeled into surgery, I gave him his penny and repeated what I had said to the others. He asked me with tears trickling down his cheeks if he could please have two. Of course, I gave him his pennies, then he thanked me and said,"You do not know what this means to me." He never explained his comment, but it did not matter since the Lord Almighty knew.

John said that at the very moment everyone had received their pennies, the atmosphere in the room abruptly changed. They did not seem as stressed as before, we just knew the Holy Spirit was present. Right before they wheeled me into surgery, I asked all of them if they had their pennies with them. They all patted their pockets and one by one they said, "I have mine". As you can see, we were having a revival in my room. Later my friends would tell me just how special they thought I was, but I tell them that it is not me, I am just a vessel of His to encourage others to seek Him.

When I woke up in the recovery room, my doctor came to talk to both John and I about the surgery. He told us that he had tried to put the port on the left wall of the chest closest to the heart, but it did not work properly so he had no *choice but to put it on the right side. I said out loud, "Praise the Lord." If he had not been able to use that side, I would not have been able to receive my port, and that would mean that every time I would go in for my treatments, they would have to use my veins. I do not have very good veins for needles, they like to roll and require numerous sticks.*

Before I began my treatments, my doctor had previously given me a prescription which required me to go downtown to one of the cancer support buildings. There I was given a bag of goodies which held three sets of different sizes of pillows that I could tuck under my arms to use for comfort and support, a wedge so that I could raise my head to help with the pain (later, I would really need the wedge for horrible heart burn), and a beautiful comfortable cotton white laced shirt that zipped up. It had two pockets sewn inside of it to use for the drainage tubes.

I was also told to go to a hospital where I could pick out a new wig that other survivors had donated. A woman came out to the waiting area and brought John and I back to one of their rooms. We were literally surrounded with so much hair, with all sorts of styles and colors. John asked the woman that was helping me where his hair was(he cuts his thin hair down every 10 days). Besides the hair, there were beautiful scarves and caps to choose from. I was allowed to choose the wig of my choice and two hats and a scarf, it was like having an early Christmas.

I had so much fun trying on everything and John remained in the room with me as I tried the wigs on. I really wanted his opinion as to which wig was the best look on me. After trying on several we finally came to the conclusion that I would be wearing home a brown wig with blonde highlights, medium length that had some waves to it. It was so different from my hair, which was blonde and straight as a poker. Once I started wearing it, I received several compliments from our friends at church telling me that they really liked it, and it was very becoming on me.

Now I was ready for chemo, or was I? On November 13, I received my first weekly round of chemo that consist of twelve treatments. Previously, my doctor had written out a prescription for a certain kind of medicine that had to be put on my port about an hour before taking the chemo, it was to numb the area. The medication in the cream was lidocaine 2.5 %

and prilocaine 2.5 %. John administered it on my port and then he had to tape a piece of saran wrap over the cream so it would stay in place, then tape it to my skin. We were not completely sure if we had done it correctly but only time would tell and besides the Lord had already assured me that everything would be fine.

When we arrived at the doctor's office we were met by such a kind and wonderful staff. It was a very friendly atmosphere, and my nurse for the day took us back to our private room, with a recliner waiting for me and a chair for John. We even had our very own television, the comforts of home. I lounged in the recliner while John remained in the chair for the entire treatment. She introduced herself with such a warm feeling of love and she made what could have been a very frightening experience into a normal doctor's visit. I had came there not really knowing what to expect and being a little apprehensive of the treatment, but as soon as she introduced herself and explained the procedure I was completely at ease.

She started taking off the saran wrap, and jokingly told us that we had gotten carried away with using it, as we only needed a small piece to cover the port. She began wiping off the cream with this certain type of cleaner that was filled with alcohol. Now, it was time to see if the cream had done it's purpose. When it came time for her to insert the needle in my port, I really did not know what would happen, but my reader's, let me tell you that I did not feel a thing except for a little pressure. The cream had done it's job, but really it was because of all the prayers being uplifted to the Lord.

So if any of you have to ever take chemo, please make sure that you ask your doctor for a prescription for this cream, it really worked great. The thought of having another hurtful needle of some kind inserted into my body was just too much to handle. Thankfully, she was able to go straight into the port without any trouble, and extracted the blood for my labs. She told us that it usually took an hour before she would hear the results. If they came back really low then I would not be able to take the chemo, so we were really praying that everything would be alright. She asked us if she could get us anything, like a warm blanket, a pillow, or anything to eat or drink? We told her yes to all the above. We were truly blessed by our Lord's heavenly people.

The way that they treated us reminded me of when I took care of my patients as a certified nursing assistant, especially the elderly. Oh, how I missed them, I gave them so much love from my heart. I treated them as my family and I never looked at my career as a job that I had to go to, emphasis on the words "had to", I was so excited just to be able to take care of them.

I had brought my pennies to give out and several copies of my first book titled "IF ONLY". They were all so excited to receive their penny and to hear that without me ever laying eyes on any of them I had thought of them and prayed for them in Jesus name. Who would have ever thought that a copper penny could touch so many lives and in so many ways. My labs came back good, and now we could begin the treatment.

The first chemo that was administered in my body was called Taxol, it was a very aggressive combination of drugs. The side effects alone would scare you to death and make you think twice about ever taking it. They consist of nausea, hair loss, sores in the mouth, muscle and joint aches, dry mouth, neuropathy in both hands and feet, diarrhea, nail bed changes, and fatigue. Shall I go on?

As I was sitting there I reminded myself that Jesus is the light that shows me the right path to walk on, so I put all my trust in Him and held on to His truth. I knew that He was going to carry me through these tough months ahead.

As the chemo was making it's way through my body, I kept myself busy crocheting prayer scarves for the other patients that I might come into contact with. John was reading a magazine that he had brought from home. I fell asleep while eating a cheese cracker and it got stuck to the roof of my mouth, John just had to have a picture of my head laying back with the cracker in full view. When I woke up he showed me the picture and everyone else. He said,"This is what your first day of chemo looks like."

Three hours later I was finished with my first round. I did not feel sick at all. It really was not that bad, or so I thought, until I got home that night. The side effects were not supposed to happen that fast since my nurse had told us that I probably would not start noticing them until around the third day.

As soon as we walked through the front door of our apartment, my head started spinning. I felt hungry so John fixed me something to eat but everything I tried to eat tasted like metal, and since I have chronic heartburn, it set in immediately. I had almost every side effect that you could imagine, except for the loss of hair falling out, that came later. Food ran right through me, I was so sick and this was only the first treatment. I still had eleven more to go of the Taxol and then I would start the more aggressive chemo. I knew the only way that I could do this was with the strength of my Savior.

There were a few days a week where I had little energy to get out of bed and walk down to the living room so I could watch television with John and my companion, Beau. But as soon as I would start walking, my body became limp like a rag doll, my legs would buckle under me and down I would go. I did not care what room of the apartment I was in, I just had to lay down, from being extremely fatigued and very weak.

By this time my heartburn was getting worse, and I was on at least three different kinds of medications to try to control it. Every time I would turn my head while I was laying down, I would immediately be hit with a wave of nausea and heartburn. Even water made it hurt in my chest and across my shoulder blades like a knife stabbing me there. I ate acid relievers all the time like candy, my heartburn was out of control. I went back to bed and laid very still, I could not move, not even a little bit.

My second treatment left me with red, swollen whelps under my skin. They were horrible looking and burned a lot. My skin looked as if I had a bad sunburn on my chest and arms, but I had not even been out in the sun. I called the doctor's office and spoke with one of the nurses, she told me to come as soon as I could get there.

We only live about ten minutes away, and as soon as we arrived one of the nurses ushered John and I back to a room. She took one look at my blotched skin and knew immediately what was going on in my body. She told us that this was one of the many side effects that can happen while being on the Taxol. She then gave me a prescription for a special cream to relieve the symptoms. The whelps continued to burn for four days, but eventually the cream did help. Finally, they began to disappear but not completely, in fact after ten months, if I look closely I can still see small blotches of red dots under my skin.

During the third treatment I had been noticing that my hair was coming out in thick strands everywhere in the bathroom whenever I would brush or wash it. One day I noticed that almost all my hair that was left came out in my hair brush. I gasped for a moment as I looked in the mirror and what was gazing back at me was a partly bald head.

I immediately thought of mom, of the time when she lost most of her hair and ended up having to have the nurse cut the rest. Our sweet nickname for her was "little head" because when her hair was not curled she had such a small head. She always had such beautiful long, curly blonde hair that cascaded down her back. I did not ever think that I would lose it that fast, and thought I would have to take several more treatments before this would happen.

After getting over the initial shock, I started to laugh out loud. It was the kind of chuckle that Santa Claus does when he says ho, ho, ho, to all the little boys and girls. A laugh that is jolly and comes from way down deep in your belly. I thought I looked hilarious and like an alien, and hollered for John to come to the bathroom, as he arrived he saw all the hair that was in my brush, in the sink, and in my hands.

This was the day that I had been dreading, one

of the times you just did not want to experience in life. I had already prepared my self ahead of time when I first heard the word chemo, since I had read it on the paper work about all the side effects. John took one look at me and said,"Babe, I think it is time." He grabbed his clippers and away he went first down one side and then to the other side. Eventually I had a mohawk, all that was missing was the warpaint. It was just like our grandson Hunter who likes to wear his hair like that from time to time, especially when he is playing sports. I think my sweetie was enjoying himself too much with those clippers.

Finally, when he had finished clipping the last hair, we stood side to side and gazed upon two round, bald heads, and we laughed hilariously. I mentioned to him that he did not have to shave his head for me like family members and friends do for their loved ones when they lose their hair. He told me that he would have done it for me anyway. I am truly blessed by him, he is the kind of gentlemen that would take care of me until death do us part.

One day while I was getting a treatment, my nurse pointed out to me a basket of hats, scarves, gloves and mask that other cancer patients had made. She told me that I could pick out two items so I chose a cute brown cap with a big brown button on the side which made it looked stylish and a colorful scarf. That was so special for the patients to take time to make all of the those beautiful apparels. I believe in that very moment I was reassured by the Holy Spirit to continue making prayer scarves. This was a way for me to give back to the Lord and to encourage others.

Pay it forward, someone does something nice for you and you in return do something nice for someone else. When I mentioned the idea to one of my closest friends, she thought it was a great idea and told me that she had some extra yarn that I could have. She gave me two bags full, and as I emptied the bags onto the bed I was completely surrounded by vibrant colors of red, blue, yellow and green yarn. As the days went by I crocheted a little, while I was trying to survive the horrible side effects. I would try to eat, occasionally I would eat a cup of delicious peaches, a bowl of cream of wheat and vanilla yogurt. I knew that if I did not eat I would be hospitalized and fed intravenously(maybe with green jello), and I did not want that to happen.

We Do Believe That Jesus Is The Light

John 8:12

When Jesus spoke again to the people, he said," I am the light of the world. Whoever follows me will never walk in darkness but will have the light of life."

7

Jesus Is Our Strength

On December 6, the chemo treatment really kicked my butt. By this time I had already lost thirteen pounds, they just kept falling off. I looked so bad with big, dark circles under my eyes. I had such a terrible time getting to sleep, in fact I can recall when I did not have any sleep for three days, before sleep finally came over me. I would try to nap when I could, and grasped at any sleep I could get. Due to the fact that I was not eating, I developed dry heaves. Everything I ate would just run right out of me.

I tell you that if I did not know my Jesus and had a personal relationship with Him, I would have been freaking out by now because of the side effects that I was experiencing. Some days Satan tried to make me feel afraid as he still does today, but Jesus would whisper to my heart," Genesis 26:24 Do not be afraid, for I am with you.

While taking my chemo I developed neuropathy. This occurs when a person has nerve damage usually in their hands and feet. The condition's symptoms consist of being weak, having numbness and pain. The chemo can cause it part of the time, this may be only temporary for some, but it has also been known to stay permanently with others. I constantly feel as if I have wadded up socks in my shoes. I have been known to take my shoes off to check to make sure that there really is not anything in them. My mom's entire family had it and some are still suffering from this terrible disease. My brother was diagnosed with it three years ago.

There were so many days when I could not even get out of bed, I felt so drained from lack of energy. And then in that same day I would get a burst of energy. Those were the very few times I could go to the park with John and Beau. Beau can not get enough of the park, running around, lifting his leg up on every tree. He is so comical that John and I just laugh at him. He is the cutest dog, and what a great companion he is to both John and I. He knew I was very *sick, there were a few days when I do not think he recognized me. But on other times he would jump up on the couch and fall asleep behind my legs. That made me feel so loved by him.*

Our granddaughter Remi, and our daughter Lisa came down several times to visit us. I remember on one occasion Remi had seen my bald head for the very first time, she looked very surprised for a moment and then, out of the mouths of babes, she told me that I was beautiful, she made me feel beautiful. She loves to play a bingo game with all the Mickey Mouse characters on it. The first time she said bingo she called it mingo instead. It was so cute, so now we call the game mingo.

Due to the treatments and the side effects we were not able to celebrate Christmas on the day we had originally planned with Lisa and Michelle's family, and that really made me sad. Because two of our daughters live close by, we were able to celebrate Christmas Eve with the two of them and their families. Anytime we can spend Christmas with our family puts so much joy in our hearts. But, on December 29 which is my birthday, two of my brothers and my sister-in law surprised us by coming down and taking *us to lunch. I chose the restaurant, Cheddars, because it has a wide variety of delicious foods, to choose from. The food and company were great and we all really enjoyed that time together.*

On January 10, we were finally able to go to Michelle's house for a delicious Italian meal of spaghetti and meatballs, salad and Christmas sugar cookies for dessert, which just so happens to be my favorite. Then it was time for the unwrapping of presents with our beautiful grandchildren. Not only were we there to open presents and to eat an awesome meal but Michelle and our son in law Nick had been remodeling their home one room at a time. We were so excited that we would finally see what they had done to it.

We enjoyed walking from room to room as they described each one in detail. It was going to be absolutely beautiful when they completed it. I had so much fun that day, especially putting puzzles together with Remi and Zoey. I played several board games with Hunter, Michelle and Lisa while John and Nick conversed with each other. I miss all of them so much. My babies and their babies are growing up way too fast. That Christmas celebration at Michelle's actually could not have come at a better time, because I felt pretty good and was able to eat a few things.

Three of our granddaughter's, Maggie, Erin and Airianna love to make art projects with me, so that year we decided to collect some pine cones to make into an ornament for their own tree. We really had a great time making those. It was a pretty good day with my health, so I was able to join in with the activities, even my better half made one. They used tiny bells, eyes that move, glitter, stickers and ribbon that made them look great. The girls were so proud of the way they turned out and they could not wait to present them to their parents.

Four days after celebrating all our Christmas's together, I was back for another session of chemo, by this time I was sick from being sick from the chemo. The nurse drew my blood for my labs before I could take the chemo. The results she brought back were horrible, and I could not take this round of chemo. My white- blood cell count was at 0, my hemoglobin was extremely low, therefore I was going to need a blood transfusion and a unit of plasma. Since I was in a very bad way with my health, I had to wear a health mask to keep from getting sick, especially when

I would be in large crowds. I just could not take the risk of getting sick since my immunity was so low, I would not be able to fight the infections. I could not even go to our large church, with tons of people everywhere. I hated missing church but we were able to watch it on the television. By doing that it made my missing church a little easier.

I was completely wiped out and I was so sick that once again I started losing more weight. I was so sick of everything tasting metallic. Would this horrible taste in my mouth that seemed to go on forever, ever go away?

My wonderful John did everything for me that week. He was so concerned about me and told me not to try to get up and over work myself. He prepared our meals and cleaned our home and everything else that needed to be taken care of. Our brother's and sister's in Christ called us and told us that they wanted to bring over a delicious meal. At one time they were dropping off food left and right, we finally had to tell them nicely that we would not need any more food. We told them that we have a small refrigerator and it just would not hold anything else, but that we really appreciated them doing this for us and the fact that they had worked so hard over a hot stove to prepare a meal for John and I. There was one time when we had so much food that we were able to share some with our neighbors in Christ's name.

By this time, because of my neuropathy getting worse, my doctor decided to forgo the last three treatments of the Taxol. When she said this, I told her I would need the weekend to really search for the answer from our Lord as to what He wanted me to do. I had already taken nine of the twelve treatments of Taxol. Our concern was if I did not take the other three would that jeopardize what we had already accomplished. Her reply was when I had my surgery my cancer was completely taken away, these chemo treatments were used for preventative measures to keep it from metastasizing to other organs such as the liver, colon, lungs and the brain. We continued to pray to the Lord and He told us it was the right decision.

Cancer is a very ugly word, but as long as we hold tight to Jesus we can literally go through anything. As before, I put everything in His care. Throughout all of this John and I continued to *stay strong in the Lord with all these temporary problems, He is our strength.*

In between my treatments, I also needed bags of fluids with nutrients they helped to build up my strength since I was not eating very much. I needed to have several blood transfusions and bags of plasma administered in my port. I thanked our Lord that my port was usable each time. Since my doctor stopped the Taxol I actually had a two week break in between the chemo treatments before I would begin the more aggressive one.

During that time food started looking and tasting better to me. Finally my taste buds were returning, it had been months and I had seriously lost a lot of weight. I was just so sick, but this break helped me to acquire the taste of food once again. I happened to mention to Cissy in a conversation that I would be getting a break in between sessions. She was as excited as I was, it was tearing at her heart seeing me so sick.

One day she called me around lunch time and said that she wanted to come and visit with John and I, and she wanted to know what she could bring us for lunch. I immediately said that I was craving White Castles. That is her and

I's favorite drive through restaurant. We share some special memories of times when we went there, such as feeding a homeless man(as always, in the name of Jesus).

I gave her our order, I think it was enough for a family, but I was really hungry. I reminded her, to please get the big red soda pop. I do not know why, but for some reason I have to have that kind of soda with my White Castles. So on that day John, Cissy and I shared a wonderful meal and a great time together.

Two days later while I was still on the break, I told John that I was craving an Arby's roast beef sandwich, with Arby's sauce and their delicious curly fries. He asked me if I wanted to go with him, because he wanted to get me out of the house for awhile. He knew that I needed a different type of scenery, other than staring at the apartment walls. I was still so very weak, but I told him I would go and we ended up eating inside. We enjoyed each other's company just as we always do, but I have something to tell you, my John does not like Arby's and he only went there because he knew I was craving them. Each bite of my sandwich, with the delicious sauce oozing out of the sides tasted so good with each bite I took, I could not get enough of it. John began to laugh and said that I must have been really hungry. He told me that he was so happy to see me enjoying my food and that once again I had an appetite, one of the very few times while taking chemo. Remember my readers, that it had been a very long time since I had craved any food. I knew that I better take advantage of this and eat as much as I could. I had to try to put some of the weight back on that I had lost from the previous months.

After the break another dreadful day was upon me, it was when I began the "red devil", this was a combination of meds called a cocktail, that was a lot stronger than the Taxol. If that was really a cocktail, I never want to drink one. I had previously asked the doctor if the side effects would be as aggressive to my body as the Taxol. She told me that I would have the same effects, but they would be much stronger, and that my neuropathy should not get any worse, but it did!

People ask me all the time, "Why you, Cindy!" "Why are you having so many trials?" I say, "Why not me!" I am being used as the Lord's vessel to encourage others." Two reasons pour out from my heart; 1) The Lord knows that I am strong enough with His Holy Spirit dwelling in me to go through these storms, 2) The Lord knows that I will use this to give Him all the glory, honor and praise, and I will go through these storms with Him as He carries me through each one. So I tell them, "Why not me, or you, or any believer!"

This new aggressive chemo not only made me sick all over again, but once again I had completely lost my appetite. I had more pain and I was extremely weak, and my energy was totally zapped from me. John said that I looked like the walking dead. Here I was again with all the nausea, pain, and heartburn. I wanted to stop after the first treatment, but as my nurse was transferring the "red devil" to my port, she reminded me of something that I had shared with her earlier in the treatments. I had told her that my faith and strength in the Lord would get me through all of this. I wondered aloud how a person that does not know Jesus could survive when they go through trials of their own, she agreed with me.

When the last drop of chemo for that day stopped flowing in my veins, my nurse brought in a cute little box that was the shape of a square called Nuelasta . I had seen this ad on the television about this medicine, so I had a little idea of what it would look like. The purpose of this box would allow patients not to have to come in the following day to get the medicine, which is a white-cell booster. Since the chemo that I was taking made my white blood cell counts very low, the Nuelasta stimulates the growth of the white-cells, which help your body fight infections. As a matter of fact, while I was taking it I had to have two blood transfusions and two bags of plasma inserted into my port.

She taped the box to my belly and it had a timer inside of it. As soon as it went off an enclosed needle poked me, but it was not that bad. I wore it home and I really had to be careful with it because of it's location and it got in the way of doing things, for example; bending over while trying to get dressed. Approximately twenty seven hours later the medication was released into my body. It lasted for forty five minutes, then I heard and felt a pop letting me know that it was finished. I immediately took it off and disposed of it in the trash. I had to have a round of this medication weekly as long as I was getting the "red devil."

Cissy had not had the chance to visit us for awhile, she was so busy preparing for her daughter, Leah's, wedding. John and I were able to attend and Leah was absolutely beautiful. The bride's dress was stunning with lots of bling on it, very fitting and it really accentuated her curves. The back was opened with a row of beaded buttons that cascaded down her back from her waist down.

Leah & Jay's first dance was just so mesmerizing. They had taken dance lessons before the wedding so their first dance was beautiful and extra special. As they were dancing holding each other so tight, they gazed into each other's eyes and you could just see how very much in love they were. They complimented each other very well.

We were all assigned tables, but we did not know anyone at first. As I was getting to know the women that were at the table, I found out that three out of the four were breast cancer survivors just like I was. It was great being able to ask them how their procedures had gone several years ago, also how their health was today. Ironically a couple of them had taken the same chemo medicine as I had and their treatments went very well. We talked about how wicked the side effects were and how we managed to get through them. Their conversations were very helpful to me.

As John & I were leaving, we sought out the bride and groom so that we could say goodbye. We are very close to the family, actually we have known the bride for many years. She and my daughter's had played together as children, we were always together. She hugged me and they both told us that they were so glad that we were able to attend. We would not have missed coming for the world and also told them that we loved them and could not be any happier for them. It was like we had just watched one of our own daughter's get married to the man of her dreams.

When Lisa, Michelle and Leah were younger, Cissy and I would take them shopping for their prom dresses. Because Leah had blonde hair like mine, everyone would come to the conclusion that she was my daughter. On several occasions the clerk's that were helping Leah to find a dress would ask me," Mom, what do you think? Isn't she beautiful?" I would tell them I thought she looked stunning, but that I was not her mom, I was her second mother. The same thing happened to Cissy when my Michelle would try a gown on and the clerk would go over to Cissy and ask her what she thought of the gown, thinking that she was Michelle's mom. Cissy would say the same thing I had said and we would all laugh about it later. The four of us went everywhere together since we treasured each other's company and had so much fun.

As I was sitting at my dining room table, trying to finish writing my book so that you, my readers, will be able to receive encouragement from it, my attacks had really gotten out of control. I had as many as eight a day, and I never knew when one would occur. The tremors in my hands caused my writing to be a sloppy mess. They were also becoming more dangerous as I was dropping things constantly. I can recall one morning as I was preparing my breakfast of cream of wheat, as I was bringing the bowl over to the dining room table it just slipped from my grasp and hit the floor hard and broke the bowl in many jagged pieces. Immediately John was there picking up the mess.

One night, John had already gone to bed and I needed to go to the bathroom. I started down the dark hallway, I was so weak and afraid that I would not get there in time. I finally made it to my short destination, when all of a sudden I started having one of my attacks. I fumbled around until I came upon the hall light switch. I grabbed the wall because I knew I was very close to falling. My hand grabbed the porcelain towel bar, I knew that at any moment it might break off in my hand. The sink, toilet and tub looked as if they were all floating around me. Everything was turning black and I could not control my body. All of a sudden, I felt something cracking in my hand, the towel bar had snapped and was jabbing me in the hand and down I went to the floor. I called for John, because our room was close by, he was there in no time at all."Praise the Lord." I believe that angels lowered me to the floor because I was not hurt at all. Even the porcelain towel bar jammed into my hand did not harm me.

Two weeks later, John took me to Cold Stone Creamy to get one of their delicious flavors of ice cream. They have so many and it is really hard to choose from them all, especially when you have to choose from their crushed candy bar toppings. As I was watching them prepare mine, I felt an attack come on quickly. Everything was spinning out of control and down I went on both knees. Other customers asked John if I needed any help to get back up into a standing position. But I told them that it was easier for me to get up on my own as long as I could get on my knees, and that is how I got up. Then I had a second siezure while sitting and eating my treat. Once again the Lord had kept me from seriously getting hurt, not a scratch.

On February 5, I went to see my doctor to get my labs done and find out what she would have to say about me losing all the weight. I was so weak that I could barely stand so John borrowed a wheelchair from another floor in the hospital. I just could not walk very far before feeling as if I was going to collapse to the floor. Every time I tried to, I felt weaker and did not have any control of my body. Upon arriving at the doctor's office, the staff took one look at me and immediately put John and I in a room and sat me in a recliner. The pain that I suffer with daily and the weakness made me feel as if I were dying. The nurse that I had that day drew all my labs and immediately sent them to the lab. John was so concerned for me, he kept grabbing my hand, telling me that he was praying for me and that he loved me.

My labs came back and once again my immunity was so low, it was at zero, which is the worse and my hemoglobin was also very low. No wonder I was feeling horrible and was going to need another blood transfusion and more plasma. Once more I had to stay away from other people as I could catch anything and I might not be strong enough to fight the germs off. My doctor said that I might not recover if I was to come in contact with someone sick.

On February 28, I got out of my bed from another sleepless night because of the acid reflex and heart burn. I tried to swallow some water and it burned my throat as it went down. I had lacerations on both sides of my tongue, on top and beneath it. I called the doctor's office to get their opinion of what I should do, they told me to go to the emergency room immediately. So John packed me up and put me in the car. The staff was very efficient and brought me to an examining room fairly quick.

The first thing they did was take my temperature, which registered at 101.8. That is way too high especially for someone that was receiving chemotherapy. Yet, I was so cold from head to toe that I could not stop shivering. Then

I inquired about receiving a warm blanket, they always make me feel warm and toasty. They told me since I had a fever, the blanket would only raise it higher.

My nurse started asking all the normal questions that they have to ask, such as," Have your medications changed? What surgical procedures have you had in the past?" I was so sick, I asked her if we could please do this another time. I was really hurting in my throat, which made it nearly impossible to talk and swallow the pills that they gave me. It felt like razor blades cutting the inside of my throat. The doctor came in to tell me that I had thrush which is one of the really bad side effects of the chemo. I was going to have to remain in the hospital for at least four days, I was sick of being sick, again.

We Do Believe That Jesus Is Our Strength

Philippians 4:13
I can do all this through him who gives me strength.

8

Jesus Is The Way, The Truth And The Life

The staff that took care of me were so kind. I believe that most of them were believers and if they were not, maybe I helped them to find Jesus through the Holy Spirit. While I was in the hospital, I called the genetic counselor to make an appointment to have my genetic testing done.

It was very important to have that done because of all the cancer that my family and I had in the past. We had been to the office previously where the counselor told us what to expect during the testing. We were so sure we could remember the floor the office was on, but of course, we got off on the wrong floor. I thought that after we got off the elevator the office would be the first door to the right, but as we started looking around the hall, nothing looked familiar to either John nor I. John saw how weak I was and that I could barely stand up. I thought that I was going to collapse on the floor, so John searched around to find something for me to sit on. I believe that the bench John found was put there by the Lord. After I sat there for a few minutes I told John that I was ready to try it again. We got back on the elevator. We were sure that we would get the correct floor this time, but once again we were mistaken, we literally could not recall what floor we wanted. By this time I was so weak I could have laid down on the floor. Finally we saw a man cleaning the windows on the doors outside of the offices so we asked him and he told us the way. Not only did he do that, but he rode the elevator with us and as soon as we reached the floor and the door opened he stepped out and got a wheelchair for me.

Once in the office we had to wait for quite some time due to the receptionist misplacing my chart. John went up to the desk and asked them how much longer it would take. He told them that I was very sick and needed to get this testing done as soon as possible so I could go home and rest. One nurse asked the other nurse if she knew what the hold up was. Finally they found my chart and took me to the laboratory where the testing would be done and the nurse was able to use my port to get enough blood for twenty eight different tests. You would not think that you could do that many tests out of two tubes.

Towards the beginning of March, I received a phone call letting me know that the results were in and I would need to make an appointment to discuss the results with the genetic counselor. I was not afraid to hear the results, because Jesus had already told me that everything would be all right since He is the Way, the Truth, the Life.

Once we were seated in her office we were told that I am carrying a mutant gene called Lynche Syndrome which puts me at a 50/50 chance for a greater risk of colon, liver, lung and brain cancers. She then asked me about how I was feeling since she told me the news. I told her that I was not worried because I have Jesus.

The gene I am carrying puts my daughters at a greater risk of the same kind of cancers, plus it also includes breast and uterine cancer. I had already had a hysterectomy when I was thirty three years old so I was not included in that risk. After talking to Michelle about this, she got in touch with her doctor who set it up for her to have the blood test performed. After several weeks had gone by and we finally heard her results, I am over whelmed with so much joy to tell you that she does not carry the gene. "Praise the Lord." If she was a carrier it would put her children at a 50 % risk also.

During the last of my chemo treatments, John and I were not able to attend church because my immune system was still extremely low. I had to wear a mask around everyone and they also had to wear one to keep me from getting sick. We would watch our recordings of church sermons in our living room. We are so blessed that our church broadcasts the weekly message for the people that are stuck at home for various reasons(this is another blessing from the Lord). But, I really missed the fellowship that we received while we were celebrating our Lord with our brother's and sister's in Christ.

I never know when one of my attacks will occur. One night I was in John's arms, where he makes me feel safe and secure. We were slow dancing, emphasis on the word slow, when I suddenly had a seizure and fainted. I was out, but I could hear John whispering my name. After

I finally came to, we thought I was doing better, but apparently I was not, because I suffered three more attacks before John could get me to the couch. I remained there the rest of the night until John helped me down the hall and into our bedroom. Every time he holds me I feel safe and loved by this wonderful, amazing soulmate of mine. When I felt strong enough to attend a church service, I had to clear it from the doctor first. At this time I was really missing my church family. It always felt good to hear a kind word or get a hug. I knew that I probably should not do any hugging, but I trusted that our Lord would keep me safe from getting sick. I had two attacks during the service and then one more in our Sunday school class. Finally I gave up, I had stayed as long as my body would allow me.

We arrived home, John parked the car and came around to my side to help me get out as he always does, he is such a gentleman. He gave me my walker and I started walking down the sidewalk that led to our apartment, when all of a sudden I started shaking and jerking from a much stronger attack. Before you knew it I was down on both knees, hitting the pavement extremely hard and falling to my side. I knew for sure that my cream, laced skirt that John had bought me the previous year for Easter was absolutely snagged or ruined, but it was not. It looked the same way it did before I put it on for church. I knew I was in a predicament as to how I was going to get off the ground without John helping me and hurting his back. I came to the conclusion that some how I would get on my knees and hoist my weight by using John and the walker. I did it, but what I really want you to know is, as I was falling, it was as if angels were lowering me slowly to the ground so I would not get hurt, and I did not. There were no scrapes, no bruises found on my body. "Praise the Lord" I could have really been hurt, but once again He was watching over me.

Because of all the attacks I was having, my neurologist and chemo specialist were working together to come up with a prescription for something to help calm my nerves. I was not nervous but they were both worried. The tremors that I had in my hands(inherited) before the chemo treatments were not nearly as bad as I was having now from head to toe. The chemo caused the tremors to be worse and now I was having one attack after the other.

The doctors finally came to the conclusion that an antidepressant might calm them down, but instead of calming me, it made me cry constantly. I had only cried around four times throughout everything that I was going through and now I was crying daily. It was like a waterfall that would not dry up. It also made my body feel weaker and I shook so much throughout the inside of my entire body. I called my neurologist and she discontinued the medication. No matter what I tried that my neurologist suggested for me to do, it did not help me. Such as meditation, listening to soft, gentle sounds of the ocean waves, the rain, or even exercises had not helped the attacks. I was still having as many as twenty daily.

March 19 was one of the happiest days of my life because it was my very last day of chemo. I had already planned ahead that I would be calling my two daughter's Lisa and Michelle so we could have a three way conversation with each other. This way it would be as if they were present in the room. As my nurse was pushing in the last drop of the "red devil" in my port, we all screamed, "Praise the Lord". I thanked Him for never leaving my side and for helping me to get through all of this.

We all hung up and John & I were waiting for my port to get flushed so we could leave, when all of a sudden the door burst open as the nurse practitioner and all the nurses came barreling into the room with party horns, throwing confetti on us. There were so many beautiful pastel colors of pink, yellow and mint green. They handed me a poster with my name on it, which said, "Congratulations, You Did It and we are so proud of you". Each one wrote something to me, I was so touched by their sentiment. As we were getting ready to walk out the door, there were lots of tears, joy, laughter and hugs. In the last six months these beautiful, kind ladies had become like family to both John and I. It was a bittersweet moment. In a way, I was really going to miss them but I was not going to miss taking chemo anymore. I knew that every six weeks I would be getting my port flushed and every three months I would be back to see the doctor so I would still get to see everybody.

I thank our Lord all the time for the special team of ladies that have and still continue to, take such great care of me during my treatments. From day one they made us feel such at peace. Really we had no idea of what to expect. One thing that I will always remember is when they told me that no matter what I needed, such as fluids and labs to be done, they would be there for me which really came in handy. I had a nurse that came to our home twice a week to help me with my physical and occupational therapy exercises. I needed to try to do these exercises to see if I could get my balance better. Up until then I was starting to regain a little strength and mobility. I could even balance on my feet with my eyes closed without holding on to anything in our very small galley kitchen. If I were to fall I would not get hurt because the oven was in front of me and the refrigerator was in back of me.

My therapist had arrived and was taking my vital signs as she always did before I started my therapies. My blood pressure registered 84/66 which was extremely low for me. Mine was usually way too high like 140/98. I had to make sure that I took it daily because my primary care doctor wanted me to call her with the results from time to time. I knew that something was not right in my body. I was so lethargic, I could barely move my body parts, every time I tried to stand it was useless. My legs did not want to hold me up. She and I together tried three times to get me out of the dining room chair where I sat earlier with John while we were eating our breakfast. When I was finally able to stand a little, John wanted to sit me down on the couch so I would be more comfortable, but I was just too weak. I really was sick. The nurse decided to call the chemo nurse. She told her what was going on with me especially my b/p being so low. The nurse said for me to get to their office as soon as I could, so John took me.

Once again I had to borrow a wheelchair just to arrive at their office, it was either that or have someone carry me. It had been awhile since I had felt like that. I had finished my last chemo treatment eight days ago. I recall that I heard them say that it was going to take time to get all those nasty side effects out of my body. Because of the necessity of the visit, I had not been able to put my special numbing cream on to help with my port. This would be the first time I had ever skipped it, but I was so sick and weak, I did not care if it would hurt or not. Besides, look at how many needles had already pricked my veins from other tests. I just wanted to get this visit over with so I could go home and crawl into my warm and cozy bed.

As she poked the needle into my port, I hardly felt any pain at all, just some pressure. While we were waiting to get the results, my nurse was already pumping fluids in me. When the results came back my immunity was at zero and my hemoglobin was extremely low. Here we go again, I had to have two bags of blood and a bag of plasma. I thought that since my chemo treatments were finished, I would not need anymore of this. Boy, was I wrong to think that.

I want to share something funny with you, on April Fool's Day my taste buds seemed to be pretty good. I was not having the nausea as before. Two of my friends were coming for a visit and they had called ahead to get our orders from Frisch's, my favorite restaurant. I had ordered a big boy, french fries and a cherry coke. I was so hungry and finally able to crave some food again. I just knew that it was going to taste good, and that we were all going to have a good time laughing and enjoying each other's company. John helped me walk into the dining room with my walker because earlier in the morning I was feeling under the weather. I was not contagious of anything or I would have had to cancel lunch with them.

I was standing there in my walker giving them both a hug and welcoming them to our home. Soon afterwards I started walking backwards really quickly, so fast that John could not catch me. Now wait for it, here comes the funniest part and I am sure that it will make you laugh. I landed on my back onto the sofa and my legs were on the arm rest, sticking straight up into the air. They had both just witnessed one of my bad attacks. I just could not help myself, my entire body was out of control. I told you that you would laugh. After I got myself up and gathered my composure, I sat there for a few minutes just looking around the room, then John helped me to stand. I told him that I wished we had video taped what had just happened and send it to the show Funniest Videos. I knew we had a great chance of winning.

Can you imagine what my friends must have been thinking? I was standing there saying hi to them one minute and then all of a sudden I vanished from their sight. I went to the dining room to eat my delicious meal, nothing was going to stop me from taking that first bite with the extra, delicious tartar sauce running down the sides of the buns (I love their tartar sauce). It had seemed like an eternity since I had Frisch's, but actually during that short break in between taking the more aggressive chemotherapy, two of my brother's came down from their homes in Ohio to visit with us and we had Frischs's for our lunch. Once again it was delicious.

The next night, while John was already asleep, our dog Beau and I were laying on the couch watching the television. I was finally feeling some sleep come over me so I decided it was time for me to go to bed. I got off of the couch and walked over towards our electric fire place heater to turn it off. I fell against it, the bricks that were supporting it shifted to the side and down I went. I had a slight fainting spell, and was in complete darkness for a few minutes.

I called for John to help me, usually I can get up on my own with just his guidance but I was trapped in my walker and was turned side ways. I could not straighten it out and knew I was in trouble. I really did not want to have to wake him but this was an emergency and I really needed him. I was halfway down to the floor, trapped inside my walker and was scared that I had hurt myself really bad. I did scrape my hand and hip on the bricks. John came to rescue me and said," Babe, are you alright? Are you hurt anywhere?" I assured him that I was okay just a few minor scrapes. He tried to help me stand but I was so weak I could not help him. My legs gave out on me causing me to fall to the floor.

I sat there for a few minutes pondering as to how I was going to get myself up off the floor. The Lord spoke to me and told me to start crawling over to the couch and hoist myself up onto it. And that is what I did. Once I was sitting there I waited a few minutes to regather my composure and strength. After John checked me from head to toe to make sure that I was not hurt anywhere else but the scrapes he let me lean on him all the way down the hall into our bedroom. I felt lifeless. John went and got our portable blood pressure machine, to check how low it was. It was extremely low 84/49.

To keep me from having to go the hospital, John gave me some crackers and the salt on them gradually brought it back up to normal. We did not fear for anything, at any time, or for any reason, because we knew that Jesus is the Way, the Truth and the Life. We put our trust in Him for everything.

One of the last remarks that my chemo doctor

said to me was that she wanted me to have an endoscopy and colonoscopy very soon since I was now at a terrible risk for colon cancer, also my mom had died from esophageal cancer. I was originally scheduled for both of them in April with my gastroenterologist that I have been a patient of his for many years. He has a terrific bedside manner and we are always joking with each other. John decided to see him also, he really likes him. Whenever I see him, he tells me that I am his favorite patient.

But before I could have those tests done, I needed to get my chemo doctor's consent. I was still very weak and the prep alone would cause me to dehydrate. She thought that I would have poor results with my blood work and she had just begun to get them stable. So I postponed the tests and told them the reason why, and would call at a later date to reschedule. She was so right to have me cancel these procedures. A month later after she examined me and read the results from my blood tests, she decided that it would be okay to have the tests done. The colonoscopy prep totally wiped me out and I lost four pounds in two days. I can only imagine how sick and weak I would have been if we had kept the original date. Once again it was our Lord's perfect timing.

Mother's day was on May13, and I want to tell you all just how blessed I felt that once again, I was free from all cancer, and would have more time to be able to celebrate life with my family and friends. To me, being a mother is one of the greatest gifts God has given me. He blessed me with my two beautiful girls Lisa and Michelle, watching and playing with them in their child hood years as they were growing up was so much fun. I loved having talent shows with them and their cousins. They would raid my closet and get all dressed up in my clothes.

Most of them enjoyed singing and took turns being the star. When it came time for me to judge the best talent I could not, for fear of hurting someones feelings, so I made them all first place winners and made sashes and a crown for each of them to wear. Another thing we used to do was have scavenger hunts in our woods surrounded by big, oak trees. This was the place that I would go to find peace and tranquility, the forest made me feel closer to the Lord.

But one of my favorite memories was when just the three of us would make a tent out of blankets. *We would act like we were camping with real food and drinks. I made a big pond out of blue poster board. It was full of fish that I had drawn and cut out. The fish had paper clips attached, we made a pole with a string and a magnet tied to it. We went fishing for our dinner in our living room.*

I loved all the beautiful hand made cards they gave me, in fact I still have most of them. Now I treasure the cards that they buy for me and I would have all of them, if it had not been for the flood in our house that we were building when we first moved to Kentucky. The rain had poured in due to an unfinished roof and drenched everything. All their drawings, their homework papers and all the beautiful cards that they had made me were water logged.

Though this caused a sadness in me, I decided to dry out the papers to see if any of them were salvageable. I did not want to loose any of them, so even though they smelled like mildew I kept the ones that were still readable. Since I married John and have my other four girls, I receive beautiful cards from them for all the holidays.

Even though this special holiday was wonderful to me, it was also a sad one, because

I still miss my mom so much especially on this day. But I know that she went home to be with Jesus and that makes me very happy. If she were still alive today I know she would have been with me during my chemo treatments.

It is now May 24, my how quickly those months had flown by. Spring is my favorite month, listening to the chirping and singing of the birds. Watching the beautiful butterflies as they flutter around and gazing at the flowers of all different shapes, shades and colors of each one. What a beautiful season that our Lord has given us, but this day was far from being beautiful for me, I had eight attacks that day.

One that comes to mind that really scared both John and I very much, was when I was in the kitchen cutting up lettuce and other vegetables for our salad, I had just put the knife down in the sink when all of a sudden, without any warning of any kind, I began flinging my arms in the air like a puppet. I was also slapping my head and kicking our kitchen island. I had never felt this kind of behavior before. John was talking to one of our grandsons on the phone, when he saw and heard me in the kitchen groaning very loudly. So he immediately told him that he was going *to have to hang up because grandma was having one of her attacks. He set the phone down on the table and came running over to me. It is a good thing that I was finished with using the knife or we both might have been seriously hurt by me flinging my arms around. I was shaking my head so fast that it gave me a terrible headache. As he held me in his arms he whispered that he loved me and told me that I was going to be okay. He spoke such loving and gentle words in my ear as he laid me on the couch and then he finished preparing our meal. I honestly do not know what I would do without him, just like I would not know what I would do without Jesus. But I know that Jesus is life and He will bring us through every storm we encounter.*

A week later I had a different kind of an attack than I had ever experienced before. I was sitting at the dining room table finishing up a chapter of my book that you are reading at the present moment, my eyes rolled backwards, then I began to slide out of my chair onto the floor, I was halfway in the chair and halfway out. If John had not seen or heard me groaning and slapping my hand really fast on the table, I could have been seriously hurt.

We Do Believe That Jesus Is The Way, The Truth, and The Life.

John 14:6

I am the way and the truth and the life. No one comes to the Father except through Me

9

Jesus Is Forever

In August, 2017 I was finally able to release the doctor that operated on my pancreas. It was a bitter, sweet moment when he told me that he did not need to see me anymore since my scans had been great for three years, and no sign of cancer anywhere. He was so kind, and gentle with his words, both John and I really liked him. He told me that I could fire him because I no longer would have to see him. But I told him that I did not want to because he was such a good doctor. He then said that I have enough medical issues going on inside my body and that I needed to focus on those.

On the way home I mentioned to John that I was going to take a picture of all my doctors and mount them on pieces of hard, poster board that would stand up. I would then take a strong rubber band and fling it at the pictures to knock each doctor down as I no longer needed them. He chuckled and thought it was a great idea, too bad we can't do that with the medications.

A couple of month's had already gone by and my attacks and my neuropathy had gotten a lot worse. Everywhere I went, it did not matter if it was church, a party or a luncheon, wherever I was I had an attack. No one seemed to be able to help me, but if I ever felt discouraged, I knew that I would not remain that way forever because of our Lord.

All of the neurologists believe that I have some hidden trauma buried deep within me, that needs to come to the surface so it can finally be released. I decided after praying to the Lord and talking it over with John that it was time for me to admit to myself that I needed outside help. So I got in touch with a psychologist whom I absolutely adore and she adores me, I could not have asked for a better one.

I was originally supposed to see another woman in the department, but as our Lord would have it, I was told that with my symptoms I would be better off seeing the one I have now.

She truly understands me and allows me to speak about my emotions. For so long I had pushed my illness's to the side. I knew that I trusted the Lord with everything, but I thought if I did seek outside help that I would hurt His feelings and it would seem as if I was not trusting in Him completely, which I was. Plus, I do not believe that I wanted to admit to myself that I needed outside help.

From the very first visit, I knew that she was the one that our Lord had meant for me to see. I have been able to open up some deep wounds from the past. Things that were very hurtful, memories that I did not want to relive. I have cried many tears in her office, tears of sadness, anguish, and joy. She is like a sister to me, she sits on the sofa with me and we share her fleece blanket. We are going through a work book together about the Functional Movement Disorder. She asks the questions and I tell her my answers. I believe that it is being very beneficial to me as I pour out my emotions with my answers.

Back in November I was introduced to the CBD oil. Four women from church came up to me at different times and told me about this *product that was known to help seizures. So since my neurologists did not know what the next step in helping me was, I prayed about the oil and heard the Holy Spirit say that He wanted me to try it. I used it faithfully twice daily, one dropper in the morning and one at night. I know it is the Lord, all the prayers that have been lifted up for me, and the oil that is making me feel better." Praise the Lord!" I am so joyful and blessed to share with all of you that I have not had any attacks since I have been taking it and I have been taking it the past three months.*

It still remains very hard for me to walk, due to the neuropathy getting worse. Lately, my feet have really been hurting, especially at night. But this is one more day and one more trial that continues to draw me closer to the Lord. This pain is not forever but Jesus is.

None of this has ever been easy, and there were a few times that I wanted to throw the towel in and call it quits while I was still taking the chemo. I just could not stand being sick anymore. But, I heard the sweet whisper of the Holy Spirit telling me that He had this under control and to remember not to give up because He is always there for me.

John was always telling me that he loved me and that together we would get through this. He kept reminding me of the scripture Philippians 4:13 I can do all this through him who gives me strength. We all need someone to build us up and keep us strong in our faith, whether it is a loved one, the Holy Spirit, or best of all – both.

There were so many times that I cried out to Him, because of all the pain and my other health issues (and I still do). I clung to Him to keep from sinking, and He has kept me so strong. I have always felt His presence. I saw a bright light at the end of the tunnel and His name is Jesus, Emmanuel, King of Kings, and Lord of Lord's. He beckoned me to come towards it, and His arms opened wide as I walked inside.

I felt such a peace and was once again reassured of how much He loves me, not just for a day but forever. He whispered to me that He had already won the battle when He died for me and you. I heard Him say that when I bring you to something, I will bring you through it. You are a child of God let me take care of you, and just be held. He brings me so much hope and peace to my soul. He is my hope for tomorrow, my peace that cometh in the morning.

Some of my family members and friends have asked me if I had to do it all over again would I. I can honestly say that as long as He is being glorified, yes, I would. I would also be able to spend more time encouraging others and loving them as Jesus wants me to do. I will not lie, I have felt cheated in some areas of my life. I felt anger, sadness and a lot of other emotions. It seems like I get a little better and then along comes something else to try to pull me down.

These mind tricks are Satan's way of working against the Lord's people. But through it all I am reminded of several scriptures. 1 Peter 4:12 Dear friends, do not be surprised at the fiery ordeal that has come on you to test you, as though something strange were happening to you. 1 Peter 5:10 And the God of all grace, who called you to his eternal glory in Christ, after you have suffered for a little while, will himself restore you and make you strong, firm and steadfast." 1 Peter 4:16 However, if you suffer as a Christian, do not be ashamed, but praise God that you bear that name.1 Peter 5:7 Cast all your anxiety on him who cares for you.

His Name Is Wonderful

Jesus My Lord

Once again He has shown His wonderful, healing power. Oh, what an adventure He has taken me on, but He has given me more strength and lessons for me to completely trust in Him and to finish the journey alongside of Him. Yes, He really held my hand as we went through the storms together. There was a lot of lightening in the storms and I could have drowned from the down pours of the trials but I never took my eyes off of Jesus, like it says in the song: Turn Your Eyes Upon Jesus. Instead of worrying, I decided from the very beginning that I would put my trust in Him, who promised me that He would take care of me. What a beautiful peace we feel when we actually feel Him carrying us through the storms of life and we believe that everything will be fine because we have Jesus.

I want to share with you what I learned yesterday through a very close friend.

Test+ Trials= Testimonies

It has been such an honor to be used by Him. For Him to have chosen me because He knew that through the guidance of the Holy Spirit I would withstand the storms and I will give Him all the glory. My readers, I pray that if you ever have to make wise, but hard decisions such as the ones I have had to make, the very first thing you do is talk to our Lord, cry out to Him and then listen to what He says. He will tell you what to do, as He has done in my life.

My honest intention in writing this book was not for you to be totally against taking chemo therapy. I went through some tough times with the chemo and He assured me of no cancer. I walked through the valley with Jesus and you can to. Just grab His hand as Satan throws another wave to pull you under. As storms came crashing over me I was surrounded by His Grace, my Rock, my Healer.

I do not know what tomorrow will bring. I do not even try to ponder on it, because I know who holds my hand. I know I will be completely healed when I get to Heaven but until then,

I WILL PRAISE HIM IN THE STORM!

Printed in the United States
By Bookmasters